A SHORT

HISTORY OF THE BIBLE

BEING

A POPULAR ACCOUNT OF THE FORMATION AND DEVELOPMENT OF THE CANON.

BRONSON C. KEELER.

THE BOOK TREE

SAN DIEGO, CALIFORNIA

ISBN 1-58509-205-3

Cover layout and design
Lee Berube

Printed on Acid-Free Paper
in the United States and United Kingdom
by LightningSource, Inc.

Published by
The Book Tree
P O Box 16476
San Diego, CA 92176

We provide fascinating and educational products to help awaken the public to new ideas and
information that would not be available otherwise.
Call 1 (800) 700-8733 for our *FREE BOOK TREE CATALOG*.

FOREWARD

This interesting book reveals that there was once a time when the books composing the Bible were not considered inspired at all, and that this idea came later. It goes on to uncover exactly who first endorsed them as inspired and why they did it.

A Short History of the Bible also reveals which books in the Bible were excluded from the canon in earlier times but are now part of it. It shows what councils excluded what books and gives the reasons why. It also reveals the identities of the men who took it upon themselves to make these "inspired" and "holy" decisions, and exactly what was at stake at the time. They are the same people who came up with the clever notion of claiming that if you failed to believe in the Bible, after it had been tailored to their liking, then you would be damned.

Mr. Keeler states that he has no specific religious agenda in writing this book, but simply wishes to expose the truth and correct what he believes is error. He is attempting to be factual instead of dogmatic. Those who are already dogmatic will not want to be bothered with facts. This book is not for them. They will keep their beliefs instead, because changing one's unquestioned belief structure is often a terrifying experience. The safety of belief is often preferred to the enlightenment of researched truth and of knowing what *really* happened during the formation of the Bible.

This book, long out of print and often suppressed, provides one with the opportunity to explore the origins and history of the Bible in a more complete and sometimes surprising fashion.

Paul Tice

PREFACE.

THE fact that no American writer has undertaken to give an account of the formation of the canon of the Bible, has left an unoccupied place in religious literature which the following pages aim in an elementary way to fill. The main purpose of the book is found in the eighth chapter, and the preceding chapters were added only as the proper presentation of the subject seemed to require them.

A popular work must be brief, for life is too short, and in these days too full of other duties, to allow much time for the pursuit of special subjects, particularly those which a separate class is supposed to be already exhaustively investigating and fairly reporting. Brevity, therefore, has been kept in view; and yet the author believes that he has substantially covered the entire ground, in so far as a general outline can do it. A few councils, whose lists, like that of Ephesus, were merely repetitions of preceding lists; and a few bishops and others, whose opinions offer nothing worthy of special notice, have been passed over in silence. But it is believed that the essential elements in the formation of the canon have been included. An outline alone—though a complete one—has been attempted; and not all has been said of each bishop and each council that might have been stated—only the substance of each bishop's views or of each council's decree being given.

CHICAGO, JULY, 1881.

CONTENTS.

"The greatest burden in the world is superstition."—*Milton*.

" Credulity is as real, if not as great a sin, as unbelief."—
Archbishop Trench.

HISTORY OF THE BIBLE.

CHAPTER I.

INTRODUCTORY.

Purpose of the Book. This is an inquiry into the origin and development of the doctrine of divine revelation, beginning with a time when the books composing the Bible were not considered inspired, and following the belief, in the light of history and approved scholarship, from its inception to the present day. In the course of the investigation it will be in order to show who first affirmed the books to be inspired, why they so affirmed, and the intellectual character of the affirmants; who, so far as is known, compiled them into the volume now denominated the Bible; what books are now included in the Bible which in earlier days were excluded, and what are now excluded which were then included; what councils of the church voted on the canonical list, what books they voted in and what they voted out; and where the theory originated that we must believe the Bible or be damned. In inviting the reader to share the inquiry, I wish to assure him that I have no theory to advocate. In opposing what I believe to be error, I desire simply to offer evidence which is easily accessible to most, which seems not to have had its due prominence in theological discussion among the masses, and which, if properly appreciated, must result in great changes in religious belief.

The Authorities. The writings of the Christian Fathers, the ecclesiastical history of Eusebius—the oldest Christian history now extant—and the modern works, *On the Canon of the New Testament.* by Brooke Foss Westcott, D. D., and *The Canon of the Bible*, by Prof. Samuel Davidson, D. D., LL. D., are the sources from which the information must chiefly be drawn.[1] As some of

---

1 The reader will observe that in many instances the references in the foot notes consist of two parts. The first is such as obtains among students. The second, which is inclosed in parenthesis, is a shelf reference to the Chicago Public Library. As a reference is provided valid in any place where the works of the early Christian Fathers are to be found, the additional one will not detract from the value of the book for the general reader, and will add largely to its usefulness for a Chicago student. The library in this city is divided into sections, lettered consecutively. section M being devoted to religion. When, therefore, such a foot note as "Origen, De Prin., l., 7, § 3 (M 1729, ll., 278)" is given, the reference within the parenthesis is simply another way of giving the first, but in terms of that library. The reader has but to go to that institution, write on a slip of paper the words within the parenthesis, the attendant will bring him the volume desired, and he can readily verify the statement. I pass thus out of the usual order, for the reason that most people lack confidence in themselves; they are not accustomed to handling ancient works, foot notes are apt to confuse them, and they think that only professional students can deal with these subjects. This is a very grave error, and has led to much abuse. I know that a class of ecclesiastics assert that the people can not hope to examine these questions for themselves, that the problems are very recondite, that only those persons who have had a theological training are competent to do it: and that the people must leave it to them to decide what is to be believed. This gives the appearance of endeavoring to ward off exposure by forestalling investigation. How-ever much the orthodox clergy may deny it, the masses are the ultimate sources of authority on doctrine. Orthodoxy itself admits this by preaching to the laity sermons explaining what the evidences of Christianity are, when they are assailed. It is fur-ther shown by the fact that when the masses cease to believe a doctrine it passes quietly out of the creed, no matter how noisily the church may have said before that it was necessary to salvation. All reform in religion must come from the laity: and if by adding these parenthetical references I shall be able to induce even a few to undertake a personal examination of the grounds of Christian theology, the end

the statements quoted from Prof. Davidson will appear to the general reader quite remarkable, a word or two in explanation may be necessary. He is an Englishman, in the recognized head and front of the Protestant students of the world. He is eighty-three years of age, has spent a life in the study of these topics, is one of the ablest if not the ablest authority now living on the subject of the canon, and is the author of *The Ecclesias.* *tical Polity of the New Testament ;* an *Introduction to the New Testament,* in three volumes; *Bible Criticism,* in two volumes; *Sacred Hermeneutics Developed and Applied ; Translation of Geisler's Compendium of Ecclesiastical History,* in four volumes; *Text of the Old Testament Considered,* and *The Canon of the Bible,* besides a great number of articles in Biblical and ecclesiastical dictionaries. He was requested by the editors of the new edition of the *Encyclopedia Britannica* to write the article on the Canon for that work, and accepted the commission, supposing that what they desired was the facts. He told how the Bible had been made up, what books had been put in at different times and what left out, and that the Bible had

will have been fully attained. The set of the early Fathers in the Chicago library is translated into English. I have used two editions of Dr. Westcott's works—that of 1875, which is not in the Chicago library, and that of 1870, which is; and two editions of Dr. Davidson's—that of 1880 which is not in the library, and that of 1877, which is. The pages of these works, inclosed in parentheses in the notes, are to the editions in the Chicago Library, and those not so inclosed are to the last editions. I give these double references for the convenience of persons who may have one edition and not the other. Each reference to Eusebius' history is also followed by the page, in parentheses, to the work in the Chicago library, which is the London edition of Bell & Daldy, 1872.

Dr. Westcott's work, *On the Canon of the New Testament,* is M 489; Prof. Davidson's, *The Canon of the Bible,* is M 88; and Eusebius' *Ecclesiastical History* is I 3331. As I shall quote these very frequently, I give the shelf references here once for all, and shall not repeat them in the foot notes.

not always consisted of just the books now in it.   When the editors read the article, they declined to publish it as it was.   They "mutilated" it, as Prof. Davidson says, and what was left after the eliminating process was completed now appears in the Encyclopedia as the article on the Canon.   Prof. Davidson then published the original in book form, entitling it *The Canon of the Bible*, and in the preface he tells why he issued it.   It is from that work that I quote so frequently.

The inexperienced person has little idea of the difficulty which the critical party finds in getting its facts before the public; nor of the systematic suppression used by the Christian press and clergy to prevent unpleasant truths concerning the Christian religion from coming out.   There is not an orthodox religious newspaper in the world that will publish the facts concerning the origin of the Bible, which are given in these pages ; there is scarcely a magazine in America that will publish them ; and it is but recently that any newspaper would do so.   Men who know the Christian theology to be untrue, have to get their audience as best they can.

Furthermore, strange as it may seem, Prof. Davidson's book was the first in English on the Canon[1] of the entire Bible worthy the attention of the student ; Dr. Westcott's was the first on the New

---

[1] By canon is meant the list of the books composing the Bible. Among the early Christians it meant the list of the books appointed to be read in the churches; and later, it came to mean the list of books which were the sources and test of doctrines. In the early centuries it was opposed to the word *apocryphal*, which last had no injurious sense, meaning simply books which were not to be read in public, but only in private, and were to be kept secret. Its present idea of "spurious" began, in a modified form, with Clement and Origen, but received its distinctive character only after the Reformation.—[Davidson, Canon, 7, 8, (7, 8.)]

Testament Canon worthy of the same attention ; and both these have been published within the past quarter of a century. One would suppose that the Christian clergy would be familiar with the history of the Bible and how it came to be compiled ; but the truth is, it is one of the subjects least understood. The Church has shown a persistency amounting almost to a method in educating the world in the wrong things. We have been carefully informed concerning the forty little children and the two she bears, Jonah and the whale, and Daniel in the lion's den ; and have been as carefully kept in ignorance concerning the things which utterly overwhelm the Christian theology.

Origin of the Books. The reader must bear in mind that most of the books of the Bible are anonymous. No one knows who wrote them, and no one knows when they were written. Who wrote the book of Judges, the two books of Kings, or the two books of Chronicles? As to their origin there have been conjectures, but the number of authors named is about equal to the number of commentators engaged in the guessing. The books in the Old Testament whose authors are unknown or disputed are Genesis, Exodus, Leviticus, Numbers, Deuteronomy, Joshua, Judges, Ruth, First Samuel, Second Samuel, First Kings, Second Kings, First Chronicles, Second Chronicles, Esther, Job, Proverbs, Ecclesiastes, Song of Solomon, Lamentations, Ezekiel, Daniel, Obadiah, Jonah, Habakkuk, Haggai—twenty-six from thirty-nine books. The time was, of course, when the Pentateuch was thought to have been written by Moses; but no theologian whose opinion is entitled for a moment to any respect, now says so. Bishop Colenso has written a work[1] proving that it was not of Mosaic authorship; but an examination of this entire question is much more readily pursued than by consulting him. The reader knows of Dr. Smith's *Dictionary of the Bible;* and McClintock and Strong's *Cyclopedia of B blical, Theological and Ecclesiastical Literature.* They are really great and exhaustive works, and are, of course, a digest of all that is known on any subject treated. They are standard orthodox volumes, they can be found in good public libraries, and they are on the shelves in many ministers' studies. The reader has but to consult one of these, under the heads of the Old Testa- ment books above mentioned, to learn that most of them were not written by the authors assigned to them; that where their authenticity is assumed by tradition, generally nothing is known of the personal history of the author; that most of them are not original works, but are, on the other hand, compilations from pre-existing records—and especially is this true of the older and more important of the books—that no one knows who wrote those pre-existing records, no one knows when they were written, no one knows who compiled them into the books which we now revere so highly, no one knows when the compilation was made; in short, no one knows anything about their origin, except that it can be very easily shown that they were not composed by Moses, and Joshua, and Samuel, and David, and the authors usually named. Orthodoxy itself long since conceded this startling fact; every minister who has studied the subject, knows it; and one of the things which provokes the hostility of intelligent men toward the Church is that the clergy

[1] On the Pentateuch, Colenso; (Chicago Public Library, M 49.)

will not tell their congregations anything about it, but keep them under the impression that such a thing has never been heard of, and that the books were written by the very men whose names they bear, and that they received them from God.

The books of the New Testament which have no known authors are Matthew, Mark, Luke, John, Acts, the Epistles to the Ephesians, Colossians, First Timothy, Second Timothy, Titus, Hebrews, the Epistle of James, Second Peter, Second John, Third John, Jude, and perhaps Revelation. The genuineness of Paul's Epistles to the Ephesians and Colossians is doubted by Dr. Davidson,[1] though the majority accept it. But this leaves ten of Paul's Epistles, and the First of Peter, the First of John, and it may be Revelation, as the only genuine writings in the New Testament. Prof. Davidson says that the Gospel of Matthew, as we have it now, could not have been written by Matthew;[2] that the present Gospel of Mark was not written by Mark, and that its author is unknown;[3] that Luke did not write the Gospel now bearing his name;[4] and of the Gospel of John he says:

"Its existence before 140 A. D. is incapable either of decisive or probable showing. . . . The Johannine authorship has receded before the tide of modern criticism; and though this tide is arbitrary at times, it is here irresistible."[5]

"No certain trace of the existence of the Fourth Gospel can be found till after Justin Martyr, i. e., till after the middle of the second century."[6]

Of course, if it were not written till 140 or 150 A. D., the Apostle John could not have been its author, for he was dead long before that. Again, Prof. Davidson says:

1 Canon, 261. 2 Introd. New Test., 1. 484 (M 104). 3 Ibid., 11. 83, 84.
4 Ibid., 11, 25. 5 Canon, 127 (99). 6 Introd. New Test., 11. 520 (M 104).

"If it be asked whether all the New Testament writings proceeded from the authors whose names they bear, criticism can not reply in the affirmative."[1]

"Textual criticism has been employed to discredit the true dates of the present Gospels (i. e., to make them earlier than they really were), and the most exaggerated descriptions have been given of the frequent transcriptions of the text and its great corruption in the second century (i. e., the believers say the evidences of the late dates are corruptions of the second century). . . . But the evidence in favor of the authors traditionally assigned to the Gospels and some of the Epistles, is still uncertain. A wide gap intervenes between eye-witnesses of the apostles or apostolic men that wrote the sacred books, and the earliest Fathers who assert such authorship. The traditional bridge between them is a precarious one."[2]

The Epistle to Titus, and the First and Second Epistles to Timothy, commonly known as the "Pastoral Epistles," were not written by Paul.[3] I have already referred to the doubts concerning Paul's Epistles to the Ephesians and the Colossians; and, in fact, some of the more radical school assert that but four of the so-called Pauline Epistles are genuine. Previous to the year 170 A. D., nothing was heard of the Second Epistle of Peter,[4] and it was not generally known till the close of the third century.[5] Dr. Westcott says that its canonicity can not even now, on historical grounds, be pronounced certainly authentic, and the most he can say for it is that it is better supported than the *Shepherd of Hermas* or the *Epistle of Barnabas*,[6] of which we now hear nothing. There has never been a time when the book of Revelation was not discarded by many persons competent to judge. The churches to which it was addressed, those in Asia, are

---

[1] Canon, 153 (120, top).   [2] Canon, 159 (125).
[3] Davidson, Canon, 239, 252, 261; Introd. New Test., ii. 193, 194 (M 104).
[4] Westcott, Canon, 227 (209).   [5] Ibid., 242 (222).   [6] Canon, 497 (469).

the very ones which rejected it. It was not in the Bibles of the Eastern Christians for more than one thousand five hundred years, and was incorporated into those Bibles less than three centuries ago. Dionysius said that many of the early Christians denounced it as being without sense or reason, and as the forgery of Cerinthus.[1] Dionysius himself did not believe it was written by John the Apostle;[2] he did not know who did write it,[3] although in another place he intimates that Cerinthus did so, and forged John's name to it.[3] Papias suggested that it might have been written by John the presbyter.[4] Caius said it was written by Cerinthus.[5] So great was the hostility and contempt for it in the East, that there is reason to believe that the bishops would not allow it to be read in the churches;[6] in the synod of Toledo, a Western church, in 671 A. D., a special decree had to be passed affirming its authority;[7] and so late as the sixteenth century, Beza, the friend of Luther and Calvin, conjectured that it was written by Mark.[8] Even yet, the Pauline authority of the Epistle to the Hebrews, and its right to a place in the Bible, have been denied by orthodox theologians. The genuine letters have the superscription, "Paul, called to be an Apostle," etc. This Epistle has none. Originally, no one claimed it to have been written by Paul. Tertullian, (202 A. D.), the Christian Father, said it was written by Barnabas.[9] In the Clermont manuscript it is to this day called the Epistle of Barnabas.[10] The Old Latin version does not

1 Euseb., Eccl. Hist., vii. 25 (281).   2 Ibid. (282).   3 Ibid., iii. 28 (103).
4 Ibid., iii. 39 (114).   5 Ibid., iii. 28 (102).
6 Westcott, Canon, 442, note 2 (414, note 2).   7 Ibid., 447, note 4 (419, note 4).
8 Pref. Apocalypsis.   9 De   dic. 20 (M 1730, vol. 3, p. 113).
10 Westcott, Canon, 263, note 1 (243, no

contain it.[1] It was added subsequently, and then as an anonymous production.[1] The early Latin Fathers, with entire unanimity, ignore it, and exclude it from the Bible. According to Origen,
some said it was written by Clement of Rome, others by Luke.
Origen himself said, "But who it was that really wrote this
epistle, God only knows!"[2] Philastrius, of Brescia (387 A. D.),
rejected it, saying that in some churches it was not read, and that its
authorship was variously attributed to Barnabas, Clement of Rome,
Luke, and Paul.[3] Grotius, in the seventeenth century, said it was
obviously not written by Paul, and he believed it was written by
Luke.[4] He also believed that the original title of the Second
Epistle of Peter was the "Epistle of Simeon," James' successor as
Bishop of Jerusalem;[5] that the present Epistle was not the original
one, but was compiled from two others by Simeon, of which the second begins at the third chapter. Dr. Westcott says to-day that the
Epistle to the Hebrews can not be shown to have been written by
Paul;[6] and Kitto's *Cyclopedia of the Bible* says that its Pauline
authorship, and its canonicity (that is, its right to a place in the
Bible) are assumptions, neither of which is admitted on all hands to
have conclusive evidence.[7] And yet, in the face of facts like these,
certain Christian teachers have told us that we must believe these
books, or be damned eternally in a lake of literal fire! That is what
unbelievers are opposing. They are not trying to tear down public
morality. They are protesting against the elevation of stupidity as
intelligence.

1 Ibid., 254 (234).   2 Euseb. Eccl. Hist., vi. 25 (232).   3 Hær., lxxxix.
4 Pref. to Hebrews.   5 Pref. to II. Peter.   6 Canon, 356 (328).
7 Art. "Hebrews, Epistle to the."

When the assertion is made that it has been proved that Moses did not write the Pentateuch, that Matthew did not write the Gospel according to Matthew, and that a particular book was not written by the person to whom it is usually attributed, the question is asked, "How does scholarship learn these things?" It is by what is known as the "historical method" of criticism. In case of a literary forgery, it is often easy to show that the work was not written by the person claimed as its author, while at the same time it would be utterly impossible to show who did write it. A few evidences that the Gospel of John was not written by the Apostle, will illustrate how the method is used.

1. The book does not claim to have been written by John. It is called the Gospel *according to* John.

2. It was not heard of till about the year 180 A. D., nearly a hundred years after John was dead. No one of the Christian writers previous to that date makes the slightest mention of it. The inference is that it was not yet in existence.

3. It came into use first among the heretics, who did not ascribe it to John. It was not until toward the close of the second century that the book was attributed to him, and then by the Fathers of the church.[1]

4. The Gospel of John says that Bethsaida was in Galilee.[2] There is no such town in that district, and there never was. Bethsaida was on the east side of the sea of Tiberias, whereas Galilee was on the west side. St. John was born at Bethsaida, and the probability is

---

[1] Davidson, Introd. New Test., II. 520, second proposition, (M 104).
[2] John, xii. 21.

2

that he would know the geographical location of his own birth-
place.

5. John was the son of Zebedee,[1] and a Jew. But the author of
the Gospel speaks of the Jews in the second and third persons. He
says the "feasts of the Jews;"[2] "the passover, a feast of the
Jews;"[3] "the manner of the purifying of the Jews;"[4] the law of
the Jews is called "your law,"[5] "their law;"[6] and he calls the
Jews children of the devil.[7]

6. The other Evangelists narrate certain miracles, and say that
John was the only one of the four Gospel writers who was an eye-
witness; yet John does not mention them. The raising of Jairus'
daughter is an illustration. This was a most astounding feat, enough
to have stunned the observer and fixed him with amazement for a
lifetime; and one would suppose that every well-authenticated case
would have been carefully preserved by those who saw it. Matthew[8] and Mark[9] and Luke[10] all narrate it. Mark and Luke distinctly assert that of the four Evangelists John was the only one
present; but the Gospel of John makes not the slightest reference
to it. The transfiguration is another. It is the only event of the
kind that has ever occurred, and therefore the men who witnessed
it ought certainly to have said something of it. Matthew,[11] Mark[12]
and Luke,[13] who were not present, describe it. Each asserts in the
plainest terms that, of the four Gospel writers, John was the only
one who saw it. Yet John does not even hint at it!

1 Matt., x. 2.   2 John, v. 1.   3 John, vi. 4.   4 John, ii. 6.
5 John, vii. 19; x. 34.   6 John, xv. 25.   7 John, viii. 44.   8 Matt., ix. 18–25.
9 Mark, v. 22–42.   10 Luke, viii. 41–56.   11 Matt., xvii. 1–9.   12 Mark, ix. 2.
13 Luke, ix. 28.

These are a few of the evidences that John did not write the Gospel now bearing his name, and they give an idea of how scholars determine the fact that a work is a forgery.

The reader has heard so much from orthodox sources, of the "unanimous testimony of antiquity to the authenticity of the Gospels," that he will be interested in knowing what that testimony is.

The first Christian writer whose works have come to us is Paul, and his Epistles we have in the Bible. He makes no mention of the Four Gospels, makes no quotations from them, and makes not the slightest reference to them. The First Epistle of Peter, the First of John, which are generally believed to be genuine, and the Revelation of John, whose authenticity is conceded by many unbelievers, do not mention the Gospels, and do not quote from them. Likewise we have the book of Acts, Second John, Third John, James, and Jude, but none of them mentions the Four Gospels, or quotes from them, or gives the slightest indication that its author ever heard of them.

The Apostolic Fathers are they who immediately succeeded the Apostles, and the first of them was Clement of Rome (97 A. D.). We have his Epistles to the Corinthians,[1] but in them there is no mention of either Matthew, Mark, Luke or John. After him comes Ignatius (115 A. D.), from whom we have four epistles, believed to be genuine. Neither of them makes the least mention of the Four Gospels. Polycarp (116 A. D.) has an epistle passing under his name. In it there is no mention of any of the Four Gospels. There is an epistle attributed to Barnabas, the companion of Paul, but probably written about 130 A. D. It makes no mention of either of the Four Gospels. And,

[1] The authenticity of the second Epistle does not affect this proposition.

finally, there is the book called *The Shepherd of Hermas*, generally conceded to be the work of Hermas of Rome, about the year 150 A. D. It, like all the other books and epistles here referred to, is devoted to doctrinal and ethical ends, but it makes no reference to either of the Four Gospels. This comprises the whole of the extant Christian literature from the death of Jesus to the middle of the second century, and not one writer mentions the Four Gospels, or makes the slightest reference to them. They make quotations from tradition and from other Gospels, but not from our four. This I shall speak of shortly. We come to Papias, the Christian Father, who lived about 150 A. D.[1] He says:

"And John the presbyter also said this: 'Mark being the interpreter of Peter, whatever he recorded he wrote with great accuracy, but not, however, in the order in which it was spoken or done by our Lord, for he neither heard nor followed our Lord, but, as before said, he was in company with Peter, who gave him such instruction as was necessary, but not to give a history of our Lord's discourses; wherefore Mark has not erred in anything, by writing some things as he has recorded them; for he was carefully attentive to one thing, not to pass by anything that he heard, or to state anything falsely in these accounts.'"[2]

The question is, Does Papias here refer to our Gospel according to Mark ?

1. We do not know what Papias said. His works are lost, and this quotation has been preserved in Eusebius' *Ecclesiastical History*. We only know what Eusebius says he said.

2. Papias preferred tradition to written records.[3] The testimony of such a man is not trustworthy. Eusebius says that he was a man

---

1 Davidson, Canon, 123 (96).   2 Euseb. Eccl. Hist., iii. 39 (115).
3 Euseb. Eccl. Hist., iii. 39 (114).

of "very limited comprehension," and that the traditions of Jesus which he collected were "rather too fabulous."[1]

3. Papias does not say that he ever saw the work. He simply mentions a tradition handed down by John the presbyter. It was natural enough that years after Jesus' death his followers should inquire, "Have we no records of his life?" and that a report should start that some one had written such a work. Later on. persons hearing the report, but finding no book, and seeing the opportunity, would write one to fill the vacancy. Just as Revelation prophesied an Everlasting Gospel,[2] and in the thirteenth century one appeared of that name.[3] Somebody saw an unfulfilled prophecy and took it on himself to make it good.

4. Suppose Papias is referring to our present Gospel of Mark; what testimony have we to the authenticity of Jesus' words as contained in it? Just this: Eusebius says that Papias said that John the presbyter said that Mark said that Peter said that Jesus said thus and so. That is the historical lineage of the authenticity of the Gospel of Mark. When the reader has that, he has it all. He knows as much of it as the best theologian does, and is just as competent to decide whether or not it is to be credited. Eusebius goes on to say:

"Such is the account of Papias concerning Mark. Of Matthew, he has stated as follows: 'Matthew composed his history (*logia*) in the Hebrew dialect, and every one translated it as he was able.' "[4]

Does Papias here refer to our present Gospel according to Matthew?

[1] Ibid. (115).　　　　　　　　　　[2] Rev. xiv. 6.
[3] McClintock and Strong, Cyclop., "Evangelium Æternum."
[4] Euseb. Eccl. Hist., iii. 39 (116).

1. He says that Matthew wrote his Gospel in Hebrew. Our Gospel is in Greek.

2. If this is Matthew's Gospel, who translated it? No one knows. The assertion of Christian apologists that the translation was by any specific persons is pure assumption. Jerome asserts that the translator was uncertain.[1]

3. There was formerly another Gospel passing under the name of Matthew, which was used by Christians.[2] How are we to know that the church has the right one? Nobody can tell.

To make the matter short, scholars admit that our Gospels of Matthew and Mark were not referred to. Tischendorf grants it,[3] and Prof. Davidson fully concedes it:

" Papias speaks of Matthew and Mark; but it is most probable that he had documents which either formed the basis of our present Matthew and Mark, or were taken into them and written over."[4]

"The canonical Gospels of Matthew and Mark can not be identified with the *logia* of Matthew, and the things *said and done* by Jesus which Mark wrote, mentioned by Papias. That writer himself does not identify them."[5]

This brings us to a period nearly one hundred and twenty years after the death of Jesus, and we have no evidence of the existence of our Four Gospels. We come next to Justin Martyr, who flourished about 150 A. D. He is really the first writer who laid aside tradition, and appealed to records.[6] In his works he frequently quotes

1 De Vir. Ill., 3.
2 McClintock and Strong, Cyclop., art. "Matthew, Gospel of," iv. 3 (1).
3 "When Were Our Gospels Written?" by Constantine Tischendorf; Religious Tract Society's edition, authorized, London, 1869, p. 107, (M 102).
4 Davidson, 124 (96).   5 Intro. N. T., ii. 520; third proposition; (M 104).
6 Westcott, Canon, 164 (147), 171 (155).

from the Old Testament, and from what appears, at first sight, to be the New Testament, and the most strenuous exertions have been put forth by Christian apologists to show that he had our Four Gospels. But they fail utterly. Justin makes three hundred and fourteen quotations from the Old Testament, and in one hundred and ninety-seven of these—that is, in two-thirds of the cases—he names the book from which he is quoting. But in making his so-called New Testament quotations, *he does not mention the name of any one of our Four Gospels.* On the other hand, he states, distinctly and repeatedly, that the book from which he is quoting is the *Memoirs of the Apostles,*[1] or the *Memoirs.*[2] He calls them "Gospels," it is true, but that signifies nothing, for there was a large number of books in circulation in the early church called Gospels, and that word, therefore, does not necessarily refer to our Four Gospels. Justin also says that he found in the *Memoirs of the Apostles,* or the *Memoirs,* "all things concerning Jesus Christ."[3] He also quotes from the *Acts of Pilate,*[4] giving the name of the book, and he refers to the *Memoirs or Gospel of Peter.*[5] Now, if he gives so often the names of the Old Testament books from which he quotes, and the names of what were to him the New Testament books which he used, why should he not give the names of the Four Gospels, if, as Christian apologists assert, he quotes from them? The inference is plain. He was not quoting from our Four Gospels. He was using altogether different books. And yet, Christian theologians have asserted in the most posi-

1 Apol. 1. 66 (M 1722 p. 64), 67 (p. 65); Dial. c Tryp. 100 (M 1722, p. 225), 101 (p. 226), 102 (p. 228), 103 (p. 230), 104 (p. 231), and twice in 106 (p. 233).

2 Dial., 105 (M 1722, p. 232), 107 (p. 233).   3 Apol., 1. 33.

4 Apol., 1. 35, 48 (M 1722, pp. 37, 47).   5 Dial., 106.

tive manner that he distinctly recognizes all four of the evangelists! I give this as an illustration of the unfairness of orthodoxy and its statements. It is a special pleader. It has an improbable theory to support—that God became a man and walked with men here on earth, and became their Savior; and, as the *prima facie* evidence of it is absolutely nothing, orthodoxy is compelled, by the very desperation of its case, to ᴗee secondary evidence where an unprejudiced mind can not see it. It even says that the *Memoirs of the Apostles* were our Gospels under a different name. An evidence that this is not true, is that Justin makes nearly a hundred quotations from the *Memoirs*, and in but two or three instances are they exactly the same as the parallel New Testament passages. There is almost invariably some difference, either in sense or construction, showing that Justin's book was different from our Gospels. Moreover, he quotes from it things which are not in our Gospels. He says that the *Memoirs* say that when Jesus went into the Jordan to be baptized a fire was kindled on the river.[1] There is no such thing in our Gospels. He says that the same devil which tempted Jesus on the Mount also tempted him as he was coming up out of the river.[2] Our Gospels say nothing of this.

The reader will find it useful to keep these facts in mind, for Justin Martyr's works are the great rallying point and battle-ground of orthodoxy. As he is the first polemical writer Christianity had. the church has made every effort to show that he was acquainted with our Four Gospels. The efforts have not been successful.

The first writer who mentions either of the Evangelists by name as

---

[1] Dial., 88 (M 1722, p. 211).   [2] Dial., 108 (M 1722, p. 230).

an author is Theophilus of Antioch, 180 A. D. He speaks of John's Gospel;[1] but he says nothing of the writer having been an apostle, simply calling him an inspired man.

The first writer who mentions all four of our present Gospels by name was Irenæus, who flourished about 200 A. D.

This is the whole of the "testimony of antiquity," to the beginning of the third century, as to the Four Gospels. The books are not heard of till 150 A. D., that is, till Jesus had been dead nearly a hundred and twenty years. No writer before 150 A. D. makes the slightest mention of them. Then come the passages from Papias, which, as we have seen, are rather the reflection of rumors than evidence of our Gospels. Justin Martyr does not mention the names of either of them. In quoting from other books, he mentions their names; and the inference is plain that he did not know of our Gospels. Theophilus of Antioch, a hundred and fifty years after Jesus was dead, makes a slight mention of the Gospel of John. But not till the year 200 A. D., nearly one hundred and seventy years after Jesus had passed away, do we hear of all four Evangelists.

After the time of Irenæus, the Gospels are constantly quoted by the Christian Fathers, and when orthodoxy speaks of the "unanimous testimony of antiquity as to the authenticity of the Gospels," it usually states how many times the books were quoted by Tertullian, Clement of Alexandria, Origen, Eusebius and other later Fathers. The Gospels were indeed quoted by them, for they all lived this side of the year 200 A. D., when the books had commenced to circulate under their present names. But those later Fathers knew no more of the authorship of

[1] Ad Autol., II. 22 (M 1723, p. 88).

the books than we do, and in fact not as much, for they had not the critical ability that this age has.   And they do not, when they quote the books, vouch for their authenticity any more than I guarantee the authorship of the letters of Junius when I quote them by their generally received title.   These Fathers simply give the names by which the books were known ; and the earlier Fathers would have given the same names if the books had been known by those names earlier.   As Dr. Westcott says:

"The main testimony of the Apostolic Fathers is therefore to the *substance* and not to the *authenticity* of the Gospels."[1]

The reader can not but have observed how few Christian writings of the first two centuries we have.   Dr. Westcott calls it the "dark age of Christian literature,"[2] so scant are its remains; and he practically concedes that the Four Gospels were not in existence up to the year 150 A. D. by saying:

"A few letters of consolation and warning, two or three apologies addressed to heathen, a controversy with a Jew, a vision, and a scanty gleaning of fragments of lost works, *comprise all Christian literature up to the middle of the second century.*"[3]

I have mentioned the fact that the Christian writers previous to the year 150 A. D. quote from tradition or from Gospels other than our four, and that the most violent efforts are now made to have it appear that these quotations are from our present Gospels.   For example, Ignatius, in his epistle to Polycarp, without intimating that he is quoting it from any book or that it is other than his own senti-

---

1 Canon, 52 (49). The italics are mine.   2 Ibid., 322 (294).
3 Ibid., 11. The italics are mine.

ment, says: "Be in all things wise as a serpent, but harmless as a dove,"[1] and modern apologists assert that this is from Matthew, "Be ye therefore wise as serpents and harmless as doves." Polycarp says: "Be merciful, and ye shall obtain mercy,"[2] and the claim is that this is the famous beatitude, "Blessed are the merciful, for they shall obtain mercy." There are a number of such passages as these, but they invariably differ more or less either in meaning or language from the New Testament parallels; and *in no instance does the writer say that he obtained them from our Gospels.* Even if the passages were identical with those in the New Testament, that would not prove the existence of our Four Gospels, for there were many Gospels in circulation in the early ages of Christianity, which contained passages identical with those now in our four, and the quotations might have been made either from one of those or from tradition. A few citations will show this. One of those early books was called the "Protevangelion," or "Gospel of James," and it was in use, though not in its present form, from a quarter to half a century before our Gospels were. Tischendorf assigns it to the first thirty years of the second century,[3] Justin Martyr quotes from it,[4] and Origen says that it was everywhere well known about the close of the second century.[5] Its name signifies its priority, *Protos* meaning first. It is still extant, and can be seen in *The Apocryphal New Testament*, a volume which contains all the Gospels and Epistles

[1] Ch. II. (M 1721, p. 259).   [2] Ch. II, (M 1721, p. 70).
[3] "When Were Our Gospels Written?" Religious Tract Society's authorized edition, London, 1869, pp. 78, 85, (M 102).
[4] Dial., 78; "When Were Our Gospels Written?" Tischendorf, p. 78 ff.
[5] In Matt., xiii. 55; Tischendorf, p. 76.

of that early time which are yet in existence, but which are not now considered a part of the Bible. In the following quotations, making comparisons with Matthew and Luke, the parallel passages are italicised to bring out the identity:

PROTEVANGELION, XXVII.

Then Joseph was preparing to go away. For there was a great commotion in Bethlehem by the coming of *wise men from the East, saying, Where is he that is born King of the Jews? For we have seen his star in the east, and are come to worship him.*

When Herod heard this he was exceedingly troubled; and, having sent messengers to the wise men and the priests, he inquired of them in the prætorium, saying to them, Where is it written among you of Christ the King, that he should be born?

Then *they say unto him, In Bethlehem of Judah; for thus it is written, And thou, Bethlehem, in the land of Judah, art not the least among the princes of Judah; for out of thee shall come a governor, who shall rule my people Israel.*

And having sent away the chief priests, he inquired of the wise men in the prætorium, and said unto them,

MATTHEW II.

Now when Jesus was born in Bethlehem of Judea, in the days of Herod the King, behold there came *wise men from the East* to Jerusalem.

2. *Saying, Where is he that is born King of the Jews? For we have seen his star in the east and are come to worship him.*

3. *When Herod* the King had *heard* these things *he was troubled,* and all Jerusalem with him.

4. And when he had gathered all the chief priests and scribes of the people together, he demanded of them where Christ should be born.

5. And *they said unto him, In Bethlehem of Judea; for thus it is written* by the prophet,

6. *And thou, Bethlehem, in the land of Judah, art not the least among the princes of Judah; for out of thee shall come a governor, who shall rule my people Israel.*

7. Then Herod, when he had privily called the wise men, inquired of them diligently what time the star appeared.

What sign was it ye saw concerning
the King that is born? They answered,
We saw an extraordinarily large star,
shining among the stars of heaven, and
it so outshined all the other stars that
they became not visible; and we know
that a great king has come in Israel,
and therefore have come to worship him.

Then said Herod to them, *Go and
make diligent* inquiry, and if ye find
him *bring me word again, that I may
come and worship him also.*

So the wise men went forth, and
behold, *the star which they saw in the
east went before them, till it came and
stood over* the cave *where the young
child was,* with Mary his mother.

8. And he sent them to Bethlehem
and said, *Go* and search *diligently* for
the young child, and when ye have
found him, *bring me word again that I
may come and worship him also.*

9. When they had heard the king,
they departed; and lo, *the star which
they saw in the east went before them
till it came and stood over where the
young child was.*

10. When they saw the star, they
rejoiced with exceeding great joy.

11. And when they were come into
the house, they saw the young child
with Mary, his mother, and fell down
and worshiped him; and when they had
opened their treasures, they presented
unto him gifts, *gold, and frankincense,
and myrrh.*

Then they brought forth out of their
treasures, and offered unto him *gold,
and frankincense, and myrrh.*

And being warned in a dream by an
angel *that they should not return to
Herod* through Judea, *they departed
into their own country another way.*

12. *And being warned of God in a
dream, that they should not return to
Herod, they departed into their own
country another way.*

PROTEVANGELION XI.

And she (Mary) took a pitcher and went out to fill it with water. And behold a voice saying, *Hail, full of grace; the Lord is with thee, blessed art thou among women* . . . .

And behold the angel of the Lord . . . . stood by her and said, *Fear not, Mary; for thou hast found favor with God.*

The angel replied, Not so, Mary; for *the Holy Ghost shall come upon thee, and the power of the Highest shall overshadow thee; therefore also the holy thing which shall be born of thee shall be called the Son of the living God.*

Thou shalt call his name Jesus, for he shall save his people from their sins.

And behold, thy cousin Elizabeth, she has also conceived a son in her old age. And this is the sixth month with her who was called barren.

For nothing shall be impossible with God.

And Mary said, Behold the handmaid of the Lord; be it unto me according to thy word . . . .

CHAPTER XII.

. . . . And said *whence is this to me, that the mother of my Lord should come to me?*

LUKE I.

28. And the angel came in unto her, and said: Hail (thou that art) highly favored; *the Lord is with thee; blessed art thou among women.*

30. And the angel said unto her: *Fear not, Mary; for thou hast found favor with God.*

35. And the angel answered and said unto her: *The Holy Ghost shall come upon thee, and the power of the Highest shall overshadow thee; therefore also, that holy thing which shall be born of thee shall be called the Son of God.*

36. *And behold, thy cousin Elizabeth, she hath also conceived a son in her old age; and this is the sixth month with her who was called barren.*

37. *For with God nothing shall be impossible.*

38. *And Mary said: Behold the handmaid of the Lord; be it unto me according to thy word.* And the angel departed from her.

43. And *whence is this, that the mother of my Lord should come to me?*

For lo, as soon as the voice of thy salutation came to my ears, that which is within me leaped and blessed thee.

44. For lo, as soon as the voice of thy salutation sounded in mine ears, the babe leaped in my womb for joy.

The reader will observe that when the different writers quote the words of Jesus or another person, they generally agree; but that in the narration of the story they differ. This shows that there may have been and probably was a manuscript in existence in those early days, containing the sayings of Jesus and others, and that this was made use of by later writers in composing their narratives. But the fact that the Apostolic Fathers use phrases or quote sayings, with the prefatory explanation, "It is written," or "The Lord Jesus says," which agree more or less with passages in our Gospels, does not prove the existence then of the Gospels. Dr. Westcott admits this:

" No evangelical reference in the Apostolic Fathers can be referred certainly to a written record. It appears most probable, from the form of the quotations, that they were derived from oral tradition."[1] [These quotations do not make it] " necessarily follow that they (the Four Gospels) were already in use, and were the actual source of the passages in question."[2]

While there is no trace of our Four Gospels previous to the year 150 A. D., and while we do not know who it was after that time that wrote or compiled them, or exactly when they did it, the testimony of the early Fathers as to one of them may throw some light on the subject. Long before our Gospel of Matthew was known, Papias spoke of the *Gospel according to the Hebrews*, and said that it con-

[1] Canon, 62.   [2] Ibid., 52 (49).

tained a history of a woman accused of many sins before the Lord.[1]
Coming down later in time we find that both Eusebius and Irenæus
agree in saying that the Ebionites used only one Gospel; but Eusebius
said it was called the *Gospel according to the Hebrews*,[2] while Irenæus said it was the *Gospel according to Matthew*.[3]   Moreover, both
Epiphanius[4] (403 A. D.) and Jerome[5] (420 A. D.) say that the Gospel
according to the Hebrews and the Gospel according to Matthew were
the same book under different names.   As the Gospel according to
the Hebrews was in existence and in use first, the deduction is quite
plain that some one subsequently forged Matthew's name to it.

1 Euseb. Eccl. Hist., iii. 39 (116).   I have already shown that the "Matthew"
spoken of there was not our present Gospel.

2 Eccl. Hist., iii. 27 (102).

3 Adv. Hær., i. 26, § 2 (M 1725, vol i. p. 97) ; iii. 11, § 7 (p. 292).

4 Adv. Hær., 13 and 30.

5 Adv. Pelag., i. 3 ; Comm. in Matt. xii 13 ; Comm. in Isai, xl. 11.

CHAPTER II.

THE HEBREW CANON.

When the Old Testament canon was closed we do not know. We do not even know that we have it all—that is, all that should be in it. The Bible frequently quotes from and refers to books of apparent authority, which are now lost. Joshua, x. 13; 2 Sam., i. 18; 1 Sam., x. 25; 1 Chron., xxix 29; 1 Kings, xi. 41; 2 Chron., ix. 29; 2 Chron., xiii. 22; Jude, 14; Num., xxi. 14, are instances of this.

The Jews had three divisions of their sacred literature, the Law, the Prophets, and the Hagiographa or "sacred books." The division, though not absolute, was substantially as follows:

THE LAW.—Genesis, Exodus, Leviticus, Numbers, and Deuteronomy.

THE PROPHETS.- -*The major prophets*, Joshua, Judges, Ruth, First Samuel, Second Samuel, First Kings, Second Kings, Isaiah, Jeremiah, Lamentations, Ezekiel; *The twelve minor prophets*, Hosea, Joel, Amos, Obadiah, Jonah, Micah, Nahum, Habakkuk, Zephaniah, Haggai, Zechariah, Malachi.

THE HAGIOGRAPHA.—Psalms, Proverbs, Job, Daniel, Ezra, Nehemiah, Esther, Ecclesiastes, First Chronicles, Second Chronicles, and the Song of Solomon.

The Jews thought most of the Law, less of the Prophets, and least of all of the Hagiographa.[1] The reader will remember that Jesus frequently spoke of the Law and the Prophets, but never of the other books. In fact, the Jews attributed little or no idea of sacredness to the Hagiographa.[2] The Christians have given a higher

---

[1] Davidson, Canon, 70 (34); Ibid., 258 (185).   [2] Ibid., 41 (46).

3

place to them than the original possessors did—than even Jesus himself did.   The idea that they were inspired did not come when the
books did, but was an afterthought.

Ezra is supposed to have founded the canon, and Nehemiah to
have finished it.   The evidence of this is slight, yet tolerably certain.
But both they and their assistants had small critical sagacity.[1]   And,
moreover, no one in Ezra's time considered any of the books except
the Pentateuch to be inspired.   The belief had not come yet.   The
manner in which they treated the volumes shows this.   If they
wished to leave out a part of a manuscript, they did it.   If they
believed they could improve a work by taking out a portion of the
author's composition and inserting some of their own, they did so,[2]
and nobody thought it wrong.   Thus, the last twenty-seven chapters
of Isaiah belong for the most part to an anonymous prophet,[3] and
several late pieces have been inserted in Isaiah's own writings.[3]   The
book of Daniel, which has been so extolled for its prophecies, was
not written till the Maccabean period, (170 or 160 B. C.), and long
after the events prophesied had occurred;[4] and the man who translated it from Hebrew into Greek added the Prayer of Azarias, the
Song of the Three Children, the History of Susannah, and Bel and
the Dragon,[5] which Catholic Christians now think as much the word
of God as any other part, but which Protestants reject.   Of course,
if the men who had the books in charge had thought them inspired
and a gift from God, they would not have taken such liberties with
them.   Prof. Davidson says:

1 Davidson, Canon, 251.   2 Ibid., 16 (14) ; 25.   3 Davidson, Canon, 33 (26).
4 Ibid., 43 (30).   5 Ibid., 44 note (30 note).

"Men of prophetic gifts wrote in the name of distinguished prophets and put their productions with those of the latter, or adopted and wrote them over after their own fashion. The fiftieth and fifty-first chapters of Jeremiah show such over-writing. To Zechariah's authentic oracles were attached chapters ix-xiv., themselves made up of two parts, (ix-xi, xii-xiv) belonging to different times and authors prior to the destruction of the Jewish State by the Babylonians."[1]

" The soferim, as the successors of the prophets, must have revised and corrected the sacred books to some extent. We need not hesitate to allow that they sometimes arranged parts and even added matter of their own. In the time of the canon's entire preparation they and the priests, with writers and scholars generally, redacted the national literature, excluding or sanctioning such portions of it as they saw fit."[2]

" From Ezra's treatment of the oldest law books we infer that he did not look upon them as inviolate. Venerable they were, and so far sacred; but neither perfect nor complete for all time. . . . The redaction to which he submitted them shows no superstitious reverence. With him *canonical* and *holy* were not identical. Nor does the idea of an *immediate divine* authority appear to have dominated the mind of Nehemiah and his scholars in the selection of books."[3]

The scribes who followed Ezra, " seeing what he did, would naturally follow his example, and would not scruple, if it seemed best, to revise the text in substance as well as form. *They did not refrain from changing what had been written, or inserting fresh matter.*"[4]

"The difference between them, (the Palestinian and Alexandrian versions of the Prophets and the Hagiographa.) often remarkable, *prove that those who had most to do with the books did not guard them as they would have done had they thought them infallibly inspired.*"[5]

This point, that the books of the Old Testament were not considered inspired when they first came into the world, is clearly proved by

1 Ibid., 38.   2 Ibid., 47.   3 Ibid., 66 (51).
4 Ibid., 34 (44).   5 Ibid., 69. Italics mine.

the fact that the Samaritan Bible never consisted of more than the Pentateuch.[1] That was the first Bible of all the Jews. When the kingdom divided in political quarrel, and the ten tribes followed Jeroboam, setting up a separate government at Samaria, they took with them their national and traditional sacred books. The hatred between them and the two remaining tribes was so great—the reader will remember that the Samaritan woman was surprised that Jesus, who was a Jerusalem Jew, should ask her for a drink of water—that the Samaritans refused to accept the other books which the Jerusalem Jews subsequently adopted,[1] and which they and we to-day hold for inspired.

When the Old Testatment was forming, divine origin was not the test of admission.[2] Other considerations were applied.[2] The questions were, "What are the doctrines of the book? What is its char acter? Who was its author? Is it orthodox?" The Bible did not form the beliefs. The beliefs formed the Bible. After the book had been formed, the process of apotheosis commenced. A long time having elapsed, and its origin having been forgotten, men began to think that because it was written of God, it had been written by God, and they said it was divine. But even then they meant simply such divinity as is assigned to human attributes or physical phenomena.[3] By 100 A. D. the new belief had grown so that none dared to add to, subtract from or alter the books;[4] and

"A belief in their sanctity increased apace in the first century before the Christian Era, so that *sacredness* and *canonicity* were almost identical."[5]

1 Ibid., 81 (62).   2 Ibid., 67 (52).   3 Ibid., 70 (54).
4 Ibid., 74 (57).   5 Ibid., 73 (56).

And by the time of Jesus so fanatical had the belief become that some persons even asserted that whoever read certain books outside the orthodox canon lost all part in everlasting life.[1]

"The degree of authority attaching to the Biblical books grew from less to greater, till it culminated in a divine character, a sacredness rising even to infallibility."[2]

The last Jewish council which acted on the Old Testament canon was that held at Jamnia, when it was declared that Ecclesiastes and the Song of Solomon "pollute the hands," that is, belong among the Hagiographa, and have no divine authority.[3] The Christian Church has since asserted that they have such authority.

In short, the belief that the books of the Old Testament are inspired did not come when the books did—it was an afterthought. That this was the case with the Prophets and the Hagiographa, we are fully aware; and judging from what we know of human nature and of how sacred books in general acquire their divine authority, we safely infer that it was likewise the case with the Pentateuch.

[1] Ibid., 59 (38) note.   [2] Ibid., 274 ff. (195).   [3] Yadayim, v. 3.

CHAPTER III.

THE NEW TESTAMENT—THE EARLY CONTROVERSIES.

While little is known of the history of the Jewish Canon, of the Christian, fortunately, considerable has been preserved, and the progress of its formation can be traced, step by step, down the centuries. After the death of Jesus, his followers increased in numbers for a quarter of a century before having any literature. Sects formed, and antagonisms arose. Then Paul wrote his Epistles to strengthen his adherents against the assaults of other Christian factions. The most violent altercations occurred, each sect endeavoring to prevail over others. Epistles and gospels and revelations were manufactured and circulated by different parties, each in its own support, and in many instances the names of Apostles, or other persons high in Christian repute, were affixed, to give greater authority. Literary forgery and piracy were not looked upon in those days as they are now. Dionysius of Corinth (170 A. D.) complained that his writings were falsified, but consoled himself by saying that the same thing was done with the "Scriptures of the Lord."[1] Mosheim, the Christian historian, says:

"There were a number of commentaries filled with impositions and fables on our Savior's life and sentiments, composed soon after his ascent into heaven, by men who, without being bad, perhaps, were superstitious, simple, and piously deceitful. To these were afterwards added other writings, falsely ascribed to the most holy apostles by fraudulent individuals."[2]

1 Euseb. Eccl. Hist., iv. 23 (149).
2 Eccl. Hist., Book i., century I., pt. ii., ch. ii., § 17, (M 248, vol. i, p. 85).

He also says that the early Christians fell into the "pernicious error" of "deeming it not only lawful, but also commendable, to deceive and lie for the sake of truth and piety."

"This vice early spread among the Christians. Of this no one will doubt who calls to mind the numerous forgeries of books under the names of eminent men, the Sibylline verses, and I know not what besides, a large mass of which appeared in this age (the second century) and subsequently. I would not say that the orthodox Christians forged all the books of this character; on the contrary, it is probable that the greater part of them originated from the founders of the Gnostic sects. Yet that the Christians who were free from heterodox views were not wholly free from this fault is too clear to be denied."[1]

The following is a partial list of the books fabricated and in circulation in that age, in addition to the ones now in the New Testament. Those in italics are preserved in *The Apocryphal New Testament*,[2] and those in Roman letters are no longer extant: The Gospel of Paul, the Gospel of Peter, the *First Epistle of Clement to the Corinthians*, Ignatius' *Epistle to the Romans*, his *Epistle to the Ephesians*, his *Epistle to Polycarp*, the Gospel according to the Egyptians, *the Epistle of Polycarp to the Philippians*, the Testaments of the Twelve Patriarchs, the Sibylline Oracles, the Gospel according to the Hebrews, the Gospel of Perfection, the Gospel of Philip, another Gospel of Matthew, the Gospel of Judas Iscariot, the Gospel of Basilides, the Gospel of Thaddæus, *the First Gospel of the Infancy of Jesus Christ, the Gospel of the Birth of Mary*, the Gospel of Scythianus, the Gospel of Tatian, the Gospel of Life, the Gospel of Thomas, the Gospel of

1 Ibid., Book I., century II., pt. II., ch. III., § 15 (p. 178).
2 The Apocryphal New Testament, containing all the extant Gospels and Epistles of the early Christian church can be had by ordering from any book dealer. It is quite inexpensive, costing not more than $1.50. It is in the Chicago public library, M 2540.

Andrew, the Gospel of Bartholomew, the Gospel of Eve, the Gospel of the Encratites, the false Gospels of Hesychius, the Gospel of Jude, the false Gospels published by Lucianus, the Gospel of Barnabas, the Acts of Peter, the Acts of Paul, the Acts of Peter and Andrew, the Acts of John, the Acts of Mary, the Acts of Andrew, the Acts of the Apostles made use of by the Ebionites, the Acts of the Apostles by Leucius, the Acts of the Apostles used by the Manichæans, *the Acts of Paul and Thecla*, the Preaching of Paul, the Preaching of Peter, the Doctrine of Peter, the Acts of Philip, the Acts of Thomas, the Acts of Barnabas, the Judgment of Peter, an Epistle of Christ to Peter and Paul, an Epistle of Christ produced by the Manichæans, the Epistle of Themison, *the Epistles of Paul to Seneca, the Epistles of Seneca to Paul*, the Revelation of Peter, the Revelation of Paul, the Revelation of Bartholomew, the Revelation of Cerinthus, the Revelation of Stephen, the Revelation of Thomas, the Revelation of Moses, the Revelation of Esdras, *the Protevangelion or Gospel of James, Thomas' Gospel of the Infancy of Jesus Christ, the Acts of Pilate or the Gospel of Nicodemus, the Epistle of Barnabas, the Epistle to the Magnesians, the Epistle to the Trallians, the Epistle to the Smyrnæans, the Epistle to the Philadelphians* (forgeries under the name of Ignatius), *the Epistle to the Laodiceans* (a forgery under the name of Paul), *the Pastor of Hermas*, the Gospel of Cerinthus, the Gospel of Marcion, the Gospel of Truth, the Gospel of Apelles, *the Second Epistle of Clement to the Corinthians*, the Gospel of Longinus, *an Epistle of Jesus Christ to Abgarus, King of Edessa, an Epistle of Abgarus to Jesus Christ*.

These are not all the books of that time. Of many we have not even the names. I have mentioned, for example, but thirteen books of Acts, whereas Fabricius made a collection of thirty-six.[1] It was from such forgery and falsification as this, with its Gospel of Judas Iscariot, Gospel of Eve, and Epistles ascribed to Jesus, that our Four Gospels (which are themselves forgeries and but a part of the common stream) came. Most of the books of that age were written to uphold or oppose particular doctrines, as when our Gospel of John is said to have been indited to refute the views of Cerinthus and the Nicolaitans.[2] Paul had to warn the Thessalonians not to be troubled or misled by letters falsely purporting to be from him,[3] and cautioned them that every genuine letter would bear his signature.[4]

While there was a great number of sects, three principal ones command the attention of the student, the Paulines, the Petrines, and the Johannines, or the followers of Paul, of Peter, and of John; a division which is maintained, in a measure, to this day. The Eastern or Greek Church preferred John,[5] and the Western, Peter. The latter divided at the time of the Reformation, and the Roman Catholic body maintained the authority of Peter as the only lawful head, while the Protestants now follow Paul. The doctrines which Protestant clergymen preach so much—predestination, foreordination, sanctification, and similar ones—are Paulisms, Jesus never having taught them. The contest between Peter and Paul raged fiercely in the early days immediately following Jesus, and each was vigorously supported by factions. Paul was the apostle of uncircumcision, and of the Gentiles; Peter, of circumcision and of the Jews. Paul wished to "carry Christ" to the Gentiles and still allow them to be Gentiles. Peter

---

1 Cf. McClintock and Strong, ACTS OF THE APOSTLES, spurious.
2 Irenæus, Adv. Hær., iii. 11, 1 (M 1593, p. 229).   3 2 Thes., ii. 2.
4 2 Thes., iii. 17.   5 Sozomen, Eccl. Hist., vii. 19 (I 3334, p. 342).

said if they become Christians they must also become Jews, be circumcised, and do as the Jews did in the ceremonial. In those days Paul was not recognized as a lawful teacher of Christianity, nor was he for more than a hundred years. In these days, if Peter should come back to earth and advocate circumcision, the strangulation of bullocks, and the strict observance of the Jewish ceremonial, he would not be permitted to preach in any Christian church, Catholic or Protestant. People do not realize how far from primitive Christianity they have gone.

Paul said, if any one, even an angel from heaven, preached any other gospel than he did, that person should be accursed.[1] He claimed authority as an apostle equal to that of the apostles at Jerusalem. But they had been appointed by the Master in person, or, eleven of them had been, and they had elected a twelfth to fill the place of Judas,[2] Peter superintending the process; while Paul had appointed himself; and for him to claim to be their equal was something to which they could not submit. Paul asked, "Am I not an apostle?"[3] And the others said he was not. Revelation (a Johannine and therefore an anti-Pauline work) says, referring to Paul, "And thou hast tried them which say they are apostles, and are not, and hast found them liars."[4] Paul claimed that he and his followers were still Jews, even if they did not practice circumcision;[5] but Peter and his friends denied it, and Revelation, again thrusting at Paul, says, "I know the blasphemy of them which say they are Jews, and are not, but are the synagogue of Satan;"[6] and

---

[1] Gal., i. 8.   [2] Acts i., 15–26.   [3] 1 Cor., ix. 1.
[4] Rev., ii. 2.   [5] 2 Cor., xi. 22 ff.   [6] Rev., ii. 9.

"them of the synagogue of Satan, which say they are Jews, and are not, but do lie."[1] Paul conceded that he had caught some of his followers by being crafty and using guile,[2] but he thought that if he had misrepresented as to his apostolic authority, since good had come of it, no harm had been done.

"For if the truth of God hath more abounded through my lie unto His glory, why yet am I also judged as a sinner?"[3]

Paul's early spirit as a persecutor appears when he wishes that those anti-Paulines who troubled the Galatians were cut off.[4] He once met Peter in Antioch, and an open conflict occurred.[5] The Ebionites, one of the most powerful of the early sects, rejected Paul, and said he was an apostate from the law.[6] The Clementine Homilies attack him bitterly under the name of Simon Magus. They reject his Epistles entirely. Justin Martyr rejected him, and scarcely deigned to notice his writings. Hegesippus would not use his Epistles, and said, substantially, that he had falsified Scripture.[7] The Paulines, on the other hand, rejected the Epistle to the Hebrews—which Christians now attribute to Paul—and they also rejected Revelation.[8] The followers of Valentinus were Paulines,[9] as were those of Marcion; those of Basilides were Petrines.[9] The Cerinthians opposed St. John[10] as well as Peter and Paul;[11] the Simonians opposed Peter;[10] the Ophites rejected St. John and St.

---

1 Rev., iii. 9.   2 2 Cor., xii. 16.   3 Rom., iii. 7.   4 Gal., v. 12.
5 Gal., ii. 11-21.
6 Irenæus, Adv. Hær., i. 26, § 2, (M 1725, vol. i. p. 97); Euseb. Eccl. Hist., iii. 27 (102).
7 Davidson, Canon, 115 (90).   8 Ibid., 118 (92).
9 Clem. Al., Strom., vii. 17 (M 1724, vol. ii. p. 486).
10 Westcott, 273 (252).   11 Epiph. Hær., xxviii. 2-4.

Paul.[1] They were snake-worshipers,[2] and claimed to have derived their doctrines from James the brother of Jesus.[3] Another sect, the Donatists, held that there were no virtuous people in the Christian church except such as belonged to their sect, and required all who joined them to be re-baptized.[4] Jerome was bitterly hostile to Origen's views, even accusing the latter, substantially, of heresy.[5] Rufinus adopted Origen's theories, and Jerome, who had been Rufinus' dearest friend, loaded him with the most terrible reproaches, until the quarrel became the scandal of the Church in that time.[5] It sounds strangely to hear persons in these days express a desire for a "return to primitive Christianity, when all was peace and love." There never was such a time.

1 Westcott, 282 (261).   2 Webster's Unabridged Dict., "Ophite."
3 Hipp. Hær., v. 7.   4 Webster's Unabr. Dict., "Donatism."
5 Ency. Brit., "Rufinus."

CHAPTER IV.

THE BOOKS AT FIRST NOT CONSIDERED INSPIRED.

As in the case of the Old Testament, so in that of the New, when the books composing it came into the world they were not considered inspired. They were looked upon the same as other books are. No one thought of calling them the word of God. The Old Testament was considered by the early Christians as inspired, and for two or three centuries after Jesus it was their only Bible.[1] The first instance of the canonization of any of the New Testament books was about 170 A. D., when, in the Second Epistle of Peter,[2] Paul's Epistles are regarded as Scripture, and that was simply a brotherly recognition of Paul after the long quarrel between the friends of himself and of Peter.[3] For a century and a quarter after the death of Jesus the New Testament was not recognized to be as authoritative as the Old.[4] And when Paul said, "The Holy Scriptures are able to make wise unto salvation through faith which is in Jesus Christ,"[5] he meant exclusively the Old Testament.[6] Previous to the year 170 A. D., wherever the early Christian Fathers used the phrase "Scripture" or "It is written," they always meant the Old Testament.[7] The name "New Testament" was first given to the collection by Tertullian,[8] about the year 210 A. D., and the collection then lacked many books

---

[1] Westcott, Canon, 55 (52).   [2] 2 Peter, iii. 16.   [3] Davidson, Canon, 134 (105).
[4] Westcott, Canon, 179 (163); Davidson, Canon, 122.   [5] 2 Tim., iii. 15.
[6] Westcott, Canon, 55 (52).   [7] Davidson, Canon, 119 (92).
[8] Adv. Prax., 15 (M 1730, vol. ii., p. 365).

which are in it now.   The word canon, as signifying a list of author
itative Scriptures, was not used till Origen's time.[1]   The word
"canonical" was used first in the decree of the Council of Laodicea,[2]
about 363 A. D.   The word "Bible" was first applied to the books
collectively by St. Chrysostom in the fifth century.[3]   And as in the case
of the Old Testament, so in that of the New, copyists felt at liberty
to change the language to suit their own ideas by taking out texts and
inserting new ones [4]   Prof. Davidson says:

"Papias (150 A. D.) knew nothing, so far as we can learn, of a New Testament
Canon. . . . He had no conception of canonical authority attaching to any part of
the New Testament. His language implies the opposite, in that he prefers
unwritten tradition to the Gospel he speaks of. *He neither felt the want nor
knew the existence of inspired Gospels.*"[5]

"It is clear that the earliest Church Fathers did not use the books of the New
Testament as sacred documents, clothed with divine authority, but followed for
the most part, at least till the middle of the second century, apostolic tradition
orally transmitted."[6]

"One thing appears from the early corruption of the sacred records spoken of
by Irenæus, Origen and others, that *they were not regarded with the veneration
necessarily attaching to infallible documents.*"[7]

"The conception of a Catholic canon was realized about the same time as that
of a Catholic Church. One hundred and seventy years from the coming of Christ
elapsed before the collection [of the New Testament books] assumed a form that
carried with it the idea of *holy* and *inspired.*"[8]

During the first half of the second century "the New Testament writings did
not stand on the same level with the Old, and were not yet esteemed *sacred* and
inspired like the Jewish Scriptures."[9]

1 Davidson, Canon, 4.   2 Ibid., 5, (4).   3 Westcott, Canon, 438 (410).
4 Tischendorf, "When Were Our Gospels Written?" Religious Tract Society's
authorized edition, London, 1869, p. 15, (M 102).   5 Davidson, Canon, 123 (96).
6 Ibid., 136 (107).   7 Ibid., 161 (126).   8 Ibid., 136 (106).   9 Ibid., 122.

"Justin Martyr's canon (150 A. D.), so far as divine authority and inspiration are concerned, was the Old Testament. . . . In his time none of the Gospels had been canonized, not even the synoptics, if, indeed, he knew them all. Oral tradition was the chief fountain of Christian knowledge, as it had been for a century. In his opinion this tradition was embodied in writing, but the documents in which he looked for all that related to Christ were not the Gospels alone. He used others freely, *not looking upon any as inspired.*"[1]

"It is certain that they [the early Christians] believed the Old Testament books to be a divine and infallible guide. But the New Testament was not so considered till towards the close of the second century, when the conception of a Catholic Church was realized. The latter collection was not called Scripture, or put on a par with the Old Testament as sacred and inspired, till the time of Theophilus of Antioch (about 180 A. D.)"[2]

Now the conditions are reversed. People in this age of the world believe the New Testament is inspired, but they do not believe the Old is.

"Two things stand out most clearly—the comparatively late idea of a cononical New Testament literature, and the absence of critical principles in determining it. The former was not entertained till the latter part of the second century. *The conception of canonicity and inspiration attaching to New Testament books did not exist till the time of Irenæus.*'[3]

"Not until the latter half of the second century (about 180 A. D.) did the present Gospels assume a cononical position, superseding other works of a similar character and receiving a divine authority."[4]

"Along with this process [the union of the Paulines, Petrines, and the other factions, about the middle of the second century], and as an important element in it, the writings of apostles and apostolic men *were uncritically taken from tradition and elevated to the rank of divine documents.* It was not the rise of new dissensions ' within the Church ' which led to the formation of a Christian canon;

1 Ibid., 129 (101). The italics are mainly mine in these quotations.
2 Ibid. 5 (5).   3 Ibid., 163.   4 Davidson, Introd. New Test., ii. 520 (M 104).

rather did the idea of 'a Catholic Church' require a standard of appeal in apos-tolic writings, *which were now invested with an authority that did not belong to them from the first.*"[1]

Tischendorf, the great orthodox scholar, in speaking of the period of canonization, says:

"It was at this time . . . that the Church . . . *began to venerate and regard as sacred* the writings which the apostles had left behind them," etc.[2]

The phrase "began to regard as sacred" indicates that before that time that regard had not existed. Canon Westcott says:

"It can not, however, be denied that the idea of the inspiration of the New Tes-tament, in the sense in which it is maintained now, was the growth of time."[3]

One of the most curious intellectual phenomena presented to the student of religious history is that of men admitting that the idea of inspiration is a growth, and still not perceiving the absurdity of sup-posing that inspiration is a fact. And yet, thousands of Christian theologians present it. There would be as much consistency in say-ing that the idea that coal is black is a growth. The color comes when the coal comes, and not as an afterthought.

We find, then, that, among the early disputing sects, it became necessary to have some authoritative court of appeal, and when the Catholic Church began to establish itself and to require such an authority, its officials, the Christian Fathers, asserted that these new books were inspired, and the word of God. But it was said simply to have authority for the new doctrines. The Fathers did not limit

1 Ibid., 168 (130).

2 "When Were Our Gospels Written?" The Religious Tract Society's edition, London, 1869, p. 95 (M 102).

3 Westcott, Canon, 55 (52).

themselves to the books now in the New Testament, but selected such as agreed with their already adopted views. The restrictions in the number of books were made later, and thus our present Bible was formed. But the Bible did not form the beliefs. The beliefs formed the Bible. Only such books were accepted as advocated the previously entertained dogmas. And the idea of inspiration passed over from the Old Testament to the New, by reason of association, proximity, and similarity of use.

CHAPTER V.

WERE THE FATHERS COMPETENT?

Since the early Christian Fathers originated the theory that the books of the New Testament are inspired, the question arises, Were they competent to do so? The popular idea is that they were learned, profound, venerable men, worthy of the highest respect; and so vigorously has this been enforced, that one of the charges on which Servetus was burned to death by John Calvin was that he had spoken disrespectfully of the Fathers.[1] The facts are quite the reverse. The early Christian Fathers were extremely ignorant and superstitious; and they were singularly incompetent to deal with the supernatural. The men who laid the foundation of the canon were Irenæus (200 A. D.), Clement of Alexandria (210 A. D.), and Tertullian (220 A. D.), and of them Prof. Davidson says:

"The three Fathers of whom we are speaking had neither the ability nor inclination to examine the genesis of documents surrounded with an apostolic halo. No analysis of their authenticity and genuineness was seriously attempted. . . . The ends which they had in view, their polemic motives, their uncritical, inconsistent assertions, their want of sure data, detract from their testimony. Their decisions were much more the result of pious feeling, biased by the theological speculations of the times, than the conclusions of a sound judgment.

1 "Servetus and Calvin," by R. Willis, M. D., London, 1877, p. 308 (M 496); Critical Essays, by Rev. T. K. Espin, London, 1864, p. 225 (E 1088). It ought never to be forgotten by the world that among the treatises thrown into the fire which consumed this great man was his work on the circulation of the blood, of which he was really the discoverer. (See "Servetus and Calvin," by Willis, p. 206 ff.) Nothing seemed to arouse the ferocity of the Fathers so much as a newly developed fact in nature.

The very arguments they use to establish certain conclusions show weakness of perception."[1]

"The infancy of the canon was cradled in an uncritical age, and rocked with traditional ease. Conscientious care was not directed from the first to the well-authenticated testimony of eye-witnesses. Of the three Fathers who contributed most to its early growth, Irenæus was credulous and blundering, Tertullian passionate and one-sided, and Clement of Alexandria, imbued with the treasures of Greek wisdom, was mainly occupied with ecclesiastical ethics. . . . [Their] assertions show both ignorance and exaggeration."[2]

Some citations will illustrate their mental characteristics. The reader is familiar with the fable of the phœnix, which was said to renew its life every five hundred years. Clement of Rome (100 A. D.) thought it had an actual existence, and he asserted that it was typical of the resurrection.[3] Tertullian believed the same thing.[4] Celsus, the noted anti-Christian writer, used this fact to illustrate the credulity of the early Christians, and Origen defended the fable rather than accept the just criticsm.[5] The writer of the Epistle of Barnabas believed an ancient superstition that the hyena changed its sex every year, being alternately male and female;[6] that a hare had as many young as it was years old;[6] that a weasel conceived with its mouth;[6] that the reason why men should eat only animals with a cloven hoof was because the righteous people lived in this world, but had expectations in the next.[6] Justin Martyr (150 A. D.) believed in demons. He said that they were the offspring of angels who loved the daughters of men;[7] that insane people (demoniacs) were possessed and

1 Canon, 156 ff. (123 ff).   2 Canon, 155 (121).
3 Ep. Ad Corinth., xxv. (M 2540, p. 123, ch. xii., v. 2 ff).
4 De Resurrect., § 13 (M 1790, vol. 2, p. 235).
5 Contra Celsum, iv. 98, (M 1729, vol. 2, p. 265).
6 Epistle of Barnabas, ch. x. (M 1721, p. 119).   7 Apol., ii. 5, (M 1722, p. 75).

tortured by the souls of the wicked who had died in their sins;[1] and that this was a proof of the immortality of the soul. He said that the food of angels was manna.[2] Athenagoras (168 A. D.) declared that the strong belief of Christians was that angels had been distributed by the Logos throughout the universe, and that they were kept busy regulating the whole.[3] Some of the angels loved the daughters of men, and fell, and thus were begotten giants, or demons.[4] These last roamed about the world, performing the evil deeds peculiar to their natures.[5] Theophilus (180 A. D.) said that the pains of women in child-birth and the fact that serpents crawl on their bellies were proofs that the account of the fall, as given in Genesis, was true.[6] Tertullian believed that the hyena changed its sex;[7] and that the stag renewed its youth by eating poisonous snakes;[8] that eclipses and comets were signs of God's anger and forerunners of national disasters;[8] that volcanoes were openings into hell,[9] and that the volcanic condition was a punishment inflicted on the mountains to serve as a warning to the wicked;[9] that demons sent diseases upon the bodies of men,[10] blighted apples and grain,[10] and produced accidents and untimely death.[11] He said that a corpse in a cemetery once kindly moved to make room for another corpse to be placed beside it.[12] He invited the heathen magistrates to "summon before their tribunal any person possessed with a devil; and if the evil spirit, when exorcised by any Christian whatsoever, did not own himself to be a devil,

1 Ibid., i. 18, (p. 22).
2 Dial., 57, (ibid., p. 164).
3 Legatio pro Christ., x. (M 1722, p. 386).
4 Ibid., xxiv. (ibid., p. 406).
5 Ibid., xxv. (ibid., 407).
6 Ad Autol., ii. 23, (M 1723, i., p. 89).
7 De Pallio, § 3 (M 1730, vol. 3, p. 187).
8 Ad Scap., § 3, (M 1730, vol. 1, p. 48, 49).
9 De Penitentia, § 12, (ibid., p. 277).
10 Apol., § 22, (ibid., p. 97).
11 De Anima, § 57, (M 1730, vol. 2, p. 536).
12 Ibid., § 51 (ibid., p. 524).

as truly as in other places he would falsely call himself a god, not daring to tell a lie to a Christian, then they should take the life of that Christian."[1] Clement of Alexandria (220 A. D.) said that hail storms, tempests and plagues were caused by demons;[2] that credulity was necessary, to render faith easy;[3] and that events in the life of Abraham were typical and prophetical of arithmetic and astronomy.[4] He kindly allowed that the Jews and Gentiles would have the gospel preached to them in hell.[5] Clement's imagination was naturally lascivious. His chapter on the immodesty of Pagan women in the bath[6] betrays the hatred of the *canaille* for the upper classes, and shows that, if a bishop in the Church could use such language, the early Christians of Alexandria must have been from the very lowest grades of society. While thus indignant at the supposed wickedness of the heathen, he wrote a book so unseemly[7] that his English editors did not venture to translate it, and in it he quotes probably more from the Bible than in any other of his books.

Origen (254 A. D.) said the sun, moon and stars were living creatures, endowed with reason and free will, and occasionally inclined to sin;[8] he was not certain whether their souls were created at the same time with their bodies or existed before, nor whether they would be released from their bodies at the end of the world, or not.[8] Their light was from knowledge and wisdom reflected from the eternal light. That they had free will he proved by quoting from Job xxv. 5;

---

1 Apol., **xxiii.** (M 1730, vol. 1, p. 99).   2 Strom., vi. 3, (M 1724, vol. 2, p. 321).
3 Strom., ii. 6, (M 1724, vol. 2, p. 17, bottom).   4 Ibid., vi. 11, (p. 352).
5 Strom., vi. 6, (M 1724, vol. 2, p. 328 ff).   6 Pædag., iii. 5, (M 1724, vol. 1, p. 296).
7 Strom., iii. (M 1724, vol. 2, p. 84).
8 De Princip., i. 7, § 3, (M 1729, vol. 1, p. 61); cf. Contra Cels., v. 10, 11, (M 1729, vol. 2, p. 278).

and that they were rational creatures he inferred from the fact that they move.[1] "As the stars move with so much order and method," he says, "that under no circumstances whatever does their course seem to be disturbed, is it not the extreme of absurdity to suppose that so much order, so much observance of discipline and method, could be demanded from or fulfilled by irrational beings?"[1] The sun, moon and stars, according to him, were "subject to vanity,"[2] and they prayed to God through his only begotten Son.[3] Famine, the blighting of vines and fruit trees, and the destruction of beasts and men, were all the work of demons.[4] Lactantius (325 A. D.) believed that demons entered men and injured them through the viscera, producing diseases and mental distempers,[5] but that the sign of the cross would drive them away.[6] As to the notion that the earth was round, he said:

"About the antipodes also one can neither hear nor speak without laughter. It is asserted as something serious that we should believe that there are men who have their feet opposite to ours. The ravings of Anaxagoras are more tolerable, who said that snow was black."[7]

"How is it with those who imagine that there are antipodes opposite to our footsteps? Do they say anything to the purpose? Or is there any one so senseless as to believe that there are men whose footsteps are higher than their heads? or that the things which with us are in a recumbent position, with them hang in an inverted direction? that crops and trees grow downwards? that the rains, and

[1] De Princip., i. 7, § 3, (M 1729, vol. 1, p. 61); cf. Contra Cels., v. 10, 11 (M 1729, vol. 2, p. 278).

[2] De Prin., i. 7, § 5 (M 1729, vol. 1, p. 63).   [3] Contra Cels., v. 11, (M 1729, vol. 2, p. 279).

[4] Contra Cels., viii. 31, (M 1729, vol. 2, p. 517). The same idea is intimated in the New Testament, Matt. viii. 31 ff.

[5] Epitome of the Divine Institutes, 28, (M 1736, ii., 111).

[6] Divine Institutes, iv. 27, (ibid., i. 279).

[7] Epitome of the Divine Institutes, 39 (ibid., ii. 122).

snow and hail fall upwards to the earth? And does any one wonder that [the] hanging gardens [of Semiramis at Babylon] are mentioned among the seven wonders of the world, when philosophers make hanging fields, and seas, and cities, and mountains? . . .

"What steps of argument led them to the idea of the antipodes? They saw the courses of the stars traveling towards the west; they saw that the sun and the moon always set towards the same quarters, and rise from the same. But since they did not perceive what contrivance regulated their courses, nor how they returned from the west to the east, . . they thought that the world is round like a ball, and they fancied . . . that the stars and sun, when they have set, by the very rapidity of the motion of the world are borne back to the east. . . It followed therefore, from this rotundity of the heavens, that the earth was inclosed in the midst of its curved surface. But if this were so, the earth also itself must be a globe. . . But if the earth also were round, it must necessarily happen that it should present the same appearance to all parts of the heaven. . . And if this were so, then the last consequence also followed, that there would be no part of the earth uninhabited by men and the other animals. Thus the rotundity of the earth led . . . to the invention of those suspended antipodes.

"But if you inquire from those who defend these marvelous fictions, why all things do not fall into that lower part of the heaven, they reply that such is the nature of things, that heavy bodies are borne to the middle, . . . but that the bodies which are light, as mist, smoke and fire, are borne away from the middle. I am at a loss what to say respecting those who, when they have once erred, consistently persevere in this folly, and defend one foolish thing by another. But I sometimes imagine that they either discuss philosophy for the sake of a jest, or purposely and knowingly undertake to defend falsehoods, as if to exercise or display their talents on false subjects. But I should be able to prove by many arguments that it is impossible for the heaven to be lower than the earth, were it not that this book must now be concluded, and that some things still remain which are more necessary for the present work."[1]

1 Divine Institutes, III. 24, (Ibid., i. 196).

The work in which this philosophy was taught was curiously enough termed "The Divine Institutes."

Cyril of Jerusalem (386 A. D.) quoted from Clement the story of the phœnix, and declared that God had created the bird expressly to enable men to believe in the resurrection.[1] He said it was a wonderful bird; and yet it was irrational—it did not sing psalms to God, and it knew nothing of His only begotten Son.[2] St. Chrysostom (407 A. D.) believed the air was peopled with angels.[3] Jerome (420 A. D.) believed it was filled with demons.[4] St. Augustine (430 A. D.) belived in demons. They tried to deceive men by persuading them that they were gods.[5] They were called demons from the Greek *daimones* on account of their knowledge. (To the early Fathers exact learning was devilish). There was also a class of satyrs and fauns called *Incubi*, to whose lascivious attacks women were constantly subject; and demons, termed by the Gauls *Dusii*, which perpetrated daily the same uncleanness. Of this there was so much trustworthy evidence that to deny it was an impertinence.[6] (So real and so universal was the belief in these lewd spirits that, in 1484, Innocent VIII. issued a Papal bull against them. And Burton, in his *Anatomy of Melancholy*,[7] expresses his firm belief in them.) St. Augustine affirms that miracles were still performed in his day. A blind man at Milan had been cured by the relics of two martyrs;[8] a personal friend of his, named Innocent, had been miraculously cured of an ailment,[8]

---

[1] Catech., xviii. 8, (M 1589, p. 243).   [2] Ibid., (p. 244).   [3] In Ascens., J. C.
[4] Epis. to Ephes., iii. 6.   [5] De Civit. Dei., viii. 22, (M 1741, vol. 1. p. 338).
[6] Ibid., xv. 23, (vol. ii., p. 92).   [7] iii. 2, (L 2162, iii. 10).
[8] De Civitat. Dei., xxii. 8, (M 1741, ii, 485 ff).

and he had seen it done with his own eyes; a lady had been cured of an incurable cancer;[1] a man in the town of Curubis was miraculously cured of paralysis and hernia by being baptized;[1] on a certain occasion evil spirits, which had afflicted some cattle, were dispelled by prayer;[1] a paralytic was cured by prayer, and by contact with a piece of sacred earth which had been brought from the spot where Jesus was buried and whence he arose;[1] a young man possessed of demons was relieved by the prayers and hymns of some women, but in departing the demons struggled fiercely, so that one, in passing out through the young man's eye, knocked that organ from the socket. It fell on his cheek, and hung there by a vein till one of the women returned it to its place, and, by seven days' praying and singing it was entirely healed.[1] A young girl, possessed of a demon, was cured by the application of oil mixed with the tears of a bishop who was praying for her.[1] The relics of the martyr Stephen had performed the most astonishing miracles, healing the blind, curing the sick, converting the impenitent, and raising the dead.[1] The eighth chapter of the twenty-second book of his great work, "The City of God," is filled with the narration of these prodigies. Concerning the theory that the world was round, he said:

"But as to the fable that there are antipodes, that is to say, men on the opposite side of the earth, where the sun rises when it sets on us, men who walk with their feet opposite ours, that is on no ground credible. And, indeed, it is not affirmed that this has been learned by historical knowledge, but by scientific conjecture, on the ground that the earth is suspended within the concavity of the sky, and that it has as much room on the one side of it as on the

1 De Civitat. Dei., xxii. 8, (M 1741, ii. 485 ff).

other. Hence they say that the part which is beneath must also be inhabited. But they do not remark that although it be supposed or scientifically demonstrated that the world is of a round and spherical form, yet it does not follow that the other side of the earth is bare of water; nor even, though it be bare, does it immediately follow that it is peopled. For Scripture, which proves the truth of its historical statements by the accomplishment of its prophecies, gives no false information; and it is too absurd to say, that some men might have taken ship and traversed the whole wide ocean, and crossed from this side of the world to the other, and that thus even the inhabitants of that distant region are descended from that one first man," (Adam).[1]

Cosmas Indicopleustes (535 A. D.) was first a merchant and then a monk. The pagan notion was gaining place rapidly in his day as to the rotundity of the earth. The belief had been that it was flat, and rested on the back of a turtle, the turtle on the back of a snake, and the snake on the back of an elephant. The Greeks had long held the theory of rotundity, and even those Greeks who came over to Christianity brought it with them.[2] The church opposed it, simply because it was Greek. Cosmas had, in his business, traveled over nearly the whole known world. He felt himself peculiarly fitted, therefore, to write on the subject, and the Christians in his time used his name, no doubt, as Christians in modern times have used famous reputations, to intimidate honest unbelief. They would say, "You believe the world to be round! Has not Cosmas gone over it? Has he not been there? Does he not know? Do you set yourself up against that great Christian scholar?" Let me urge upon the reader never to yield to the pernicious habit of fearing simply a great name.

1 Ibid., xvi. 9, (M 1741, II. 1180).
2 Athenagoras, for example: Legatio pro Christ., viii. (M 1722, p. 383).

It and scholarship do not, by any means, always go together; and the only way by which enlightenment and civilization can possibly make progress is through the determination of each individual member of society, no matter how humble he may be, to do his own thinking on all subjects where one man's thought is as good as another's—and such is the case in theology—and, when he knows that he is right, to stand by it, though all the world be against him. One reason for the intolerable slowness with which men have escaped from the superstitions of theology is, they have allowed themselves to be overawed with the names of Augustine, Jerome, Calvin, and other supposedly great thinkers, who were, in fact, utterly incompetent to deal with the questions which they handled.

Cosmas, seeing the "wave of infidelity sweeping over the land" concerning the flatness of the earth, wrote a work to counteract it. He called it "Christian Topography," and said it was "intended to denounce the false and heathen doctrine of the rotundity of the earth," and was to be a "Christian description of the universe, established by demonstrations from Divine Scripture, concerning which it is not lawful for a Christian to doubt." According to him the world is a rectangular plane, twice as long as broad. The heavens come down to the earth on the four sides, like the walls of a room. The earth lies in the center, with the ocean all about it. Beyond the ocean lies the untraversed land, the terrestrial paradise. On the north side of the earth is a mountain behind which the sun sets. (Cosmas lived in Egypt, where the sun seems to set in the north.) The plane of the earth was not exactly horizontal, but inclined slightly from the north, for which reason the Euphrates, the Tigris, and other rivers running southward, are rapid, while the Nile, and others running northward, are slow. People who believed the earth to be round were blasphemers, given up for their sins to belief in that impudent nonsense.[1]

Similar science was taught by Patricius, Diodorus of Tarsus and other Nestorian theologians. The Christian religion staked its all on the flatness of the earth's surface, and when science proved the rotundity, theology was dealt a blow from which it can never recover. Truly is it said, "Theology ever has been, as it ever must be, the barbarian's interpretation of the universe."

Gregory the Great (600 A. D.) believed that volcanoes were the entrances to hell, and he tells a story of Theodoric and Pope John being cast, in chains, through the mouth of one of them, into the lower regions.[2] Two nuns, who had been excommunicated for talking too much, were buried in the earthen floor of the church. When the deacon, in saying mass, commanded all suspended persons to leave the edifice, the two nuns would arise from their graves and depart, to return after the mass was over. Many persons had seen these resurrections, and the nuns continued them till they learned to hold their tongues, when the ban was removed, and they rested peacefully in their tombs.[3] A dead child was once raised to life simply by having a stocking, the relic of a holy man, placed on its bosom.[4] Having no oil, lamps were fed with water, and wicked with paper, and they burned perfectly.[5] A city was on fire, and nothing could stay the ravages till Bishop Marcellinus threw himself against the

---

[1] Ency. Brit., "Cosmas." A very good description of "Christian Topography" will also be found in Lecky's History of Rationalism, i. 276 ff. (L. 2145).

[2] Dial., iv. 30. (M 1498, p. 253).   [3] Ibid., ii. 23 (p. 96).

[4] Ibid., i. 2 (p. 12).   [5] Ibid., i. 5 (p. 25).

flames, and they were immediately extinguished.[1] A huge stone, which five hundred yoke of oxen could not stir, was removed a long distance by prayer.[2] A lamp, shattered to fragments, was mended perfectly,[2] and exhausted oil vessels were filled; a certain monk died,[3] and predestination was fulfilled,[4] all in answer to prayer. Gregory's *Dialogues* are filled with such narrations, and Henry James Coleridge, his biographer, says he was a "great man," a "great saint," and that he "towered above his contemporaries and their immediate predecessors and followers."

St. Thomas Aquinas (1270 A. D) affirmed that diseases and tempests were the direct work of the devil,[5] and Justin Martyr, Theoph ilus of Antioch, Athenagoras, Tatian, Cyprian of Carthage, Tertullian, Origen, Jerome, Lactantius, Eusebius—in fact, all the early Christians believed in demons. The New Testament writers believed in them. The air was peopled with them and with angels. Every fountain, every tree, every stream, every grove had its sprite. Everything that was done must be done under a miracle. The Almighty had to be invoked to perform the simplest things. Nothing was too great for the credulity of the Fathers, provided only it was improbable; and nothing small enough for belief, if it was at all probable.

The erroneous and grotesque beliefs of the Christian Fathers could be quoted until they filled a large volume, but these few will illustrate the intellectual condition of the ages which originated and transmitted the Bible to us. It will be said that the Fathers were as good as their times. That can not be maintained. They were not

1 Ibid., 1. 6 (p. 28). 2 Ibid., 1. 7 (p. 29). 3 Ibid., 1. 8 (p. 32).
4 Ibid., 1. 8 (p. 33). 5 Summa Theolog., quæst. 80, § 2.

even as good. There were men in those days who saw that the world
was round. The fact that Augustine, Lactantius, and other Fathers,
opposed the theory, shows that there were men who advocated it.
In the quotations given above from Lactantius and Augustine, they
recite quite fully the arguments which prove that the world was
round. Yet the writers could not see that the arguments were valid,
whereas other men could. In short, the sum of the charge against
the Fathers is that they were not competent to tell what was evidence
of a fact and what was not. They cited as evidence of a theory
things which are not in the slightest degree such, and they would
look directly into the face of evidence which established theories they
did not endorse, and would still be unable to see that it was evidence.
Now, if the Fathers were great scholars, they should not have been
so persistently in the wrong. They should have seen the truth at
least as easily as the others did. What has become of the names and
memories of the men who in those days stood up for the truth? Are
they even yet called great? The Christian Church has been hon-
oring the wrong persons.

Moreover, admitting, for the sake of the argument, that these Christian Fathers were as great as their time, we deny that they or their
age were competent to form a Bible for this age.

But one apology has ever been made for these remarkable errors
of the Fathers, and that is "spiritual insight." Christian defenders
say that, while the Fathers were ignorant, and even superstitious,
they were yet "gifted with great spiritual insight." This term signifies the possibility of perceiving something which does not exist and
where it does not exist. It is synonymous with "unlimited credulity."

Not alone in nature, but also in literature, the Fathers were igno-rant and unscholarly. Jerome and Origen were the only ones who could read Hebrew,[1] unless we except Dorotheus.[2] Justin Martyr quotes from Jeremiah and calls it Isaiah.[3] Clement of Alexandria quotes as Scripture passages which are not in the Bible.[4] He quotes as Paul's, words which are not in Paul.[5] In quoting from an oppo-nent he would insert—not with intent to misrepresent, perhaps, but with the same result—words not in the original,[6] and he even does the same in quoting from the Bible.[7] Tertullian quotes as in Levit-icus a passage not in that book;[8] he misquotes history;[9] he cites as in Isaiah a passage not in that book, but in Revelation,[10] and he is frequently inaccurate in quotations. The Gospel writers committed the same blunders. The man who wrote the Gospel of Matthew attributes to Jeremiah[11] a passage which is in Zechariah;[12] and the writer of the Gospel of Mark attributes to Isaiah[13] a passage which is in Malachi.[14] One curious illustration of this, and of how sacred books are formed, is seen in the excess of the Catholic over the Protestant Bible. The former has quite a number of books which are not in the latter—such as the two of Maccabees and the Song of the Three Children—which Protestants call the apocryphal Old Testa-

---

[1] Davidson, Canon, 170 (133).

[2] Euseb. Eccl. Hist. vii. 32 (294).   [3] Apol. 1. 54. (M 1722. p. 53).

[4] Strom., ii. 6 (M 1724, vol. 2, p. 18); ii. 15, (p. 42); ibid., (p. 43); vii. 13, (p. 467); vii. 16, p. 477).

[5] Strom., vi. 5 (M 1724, vol. 2, p. 328).   [6] Strom., ii. 4 (1724, vol. 2, p. 11, note).

[7] Strom., iv. 26 (M 1724, vol. 2, p. 218).   [8] On Chastity, vii. (M 1730, vol. 3, p. 11).

[9] On Monogamy, vi. (M 1730, vol. 3, p. 31). [10] On Modesty, vi. (M 1730, vol. 3, p. 67).

[11] Matt., xxvii. 9.   [12] Zech., xi. 12-13.

[13] Mark, i. 2. The early manuscripts insert the name of Isaiah as the authority, but the later ones omitted it because it was such a clear error.

[14] Mal., iii. 1.

ment, but which Catholics consider as much the word of God as any other books.   The reader has already seen that the ancient Jews did not consider these authoritative, and the Palestinian Jews did not include them in the sacred collection.   The Greek Jews, however, thought more of them, and the Alexandrian Jews placed them in an appendix to the Greek canons at the end of their Bibles, the same as they used to be printed in our old Bibles.   The early Christians of Africa could not read Hebrew; they had to use the Greek manuscripts; and as they saw the apocryphal books in the collection, they supposed they were a part of it.   The result was that the early Bible-makers in the African church included the apocryphal books because they were not intelligent enough to leave them out.[1] St. Augustine included them because he found them there, and the Catholic Church retained them because St. Augustine did.

[1] This is hinted at by Prof. Davidson, Canon, 83 (64).

CHAPTER VI.

THE FATHERS QUOTED AS SCRIPTURE BOOKS WHICH ARE NOW CALLED APOCRYPHAL.

The early Christian Fathers, then, originated the theory that the books now in the New Testament were inspired. They did this to have an authority to which they might appeal in support of the newly-forming doctrines. The necessity for such an authority caused them to think and say they had one. But in determining the books to be honored with that position they also designated a number which are not now in the Bible. Nor was their idea of inspiration so illogical as ours. They had in mind a mild type, such as we concede to Shakespeare or Milton, and when they said the books were divine, they meant much the same as we do when we say that Homer and Dante are divine. And it is very necessary to keep in mind that Biblical criticism or scholarship scarcely existed in the first three centuries,[1] when the New Testament was founded. A few citations will show how widely the early Fathers' ideas differed from ours as to what books are inspired.

The reader remembers the *Sibylline books*. A certain old woman appeared before Tarquin, king of Rome, and offered to sell him nine volumes. Upon his refusal to purchase, she departed, burned three, and offered the remaining six for the original price. He still refused, whereupon she burned three more, and demanded the original price

---

[1] Davidson, Canon, 252, bottom.

for the last three.   The King's curiosity was aroused; he purchased the books, and the Sibyl vanished.   The volumes were carefully kept in a stone chest; priests were appointed to interpret them, and they became the Bible of the Romans.[1]   They perished in the fire which destroyed the temple of Jupiter Capitolinus, and were replaced by collection from other temples; just as when, on a certain occasion, all the copies of the Pentateuch were burned up, Ezra replaced them by rewriting.[2] In the time of Jesus these Sibylline books had the highest authority in the Roman Empire.   Naturally the early Chris tian writers fell into the then prevalent custom of using them; but they went further, and appropriated them to their own religion.   Mos heim says, in the passage which I have quoted from him, that they were among the forgeries of the first two centuries. But Justin Martyr quotes them with as much authority as he does Moses and the prophets.[3] Clement of Alexandria cites the Sibyl as a prophetess,[4] calls her the prophetess of the Hebrews,[5] and quotes the Pentateuch and the Sibylline books in the same sentence.[6] Lactantius, in his "Divine Institutes," quotes them.[7] In the same way Hegesippus used the *Gospel according to the Hebrews* and the *Syriac Gospel.*[8] The *Gospel according to the Hebrews* is quoted by Clement of Alexandria with quite as much respect as any other gospel.[9] Origen frequently cites it.[10] Jerome does the same thing.[11] The Clementine Homilies (161–180 A. D.)

[1] Dictionary of Greek and Roman Antiquities, "Sibyllini Libri."
[2] 2 Esdras, xiv. 21 ff.   [3] Apol., i. 20 (M 1722, p. 24); i. 44 (M 1722, p. 45).
[4] Exhort., ii. (M 1724, vol. 1, p. 36); iv. (p. 55); viii. (p. 76).
[5] Ibid., vi. (p. 72).   [6] Ibid., iv. (p. 64).
[7] i. 6, 7 (M 1736, i. p. 14 ff.); vii. 15 (M 1736, i. 465); vii. 19 (M 1736, i. 471).
[8] Euseb. Eccl. Hist., iv. 22 (p. 146).   [9] Strom., ii. 9 (M 1724, ii. 28)
[10] e. g., In Joh., vol. 4, 63; Matt. xix. 19, vol. 3, p. 771.   [11] De Vir. Ill., 2.

used the *Gospel according to the Egyptians*,[1] and Clement of Alexandria cites it.[2] Barnabas quotes the book of *Enoch* as Scripture.[3] So does Tertullian,[4] and he defended its genuineness with an argument which has furnished amusement for the wits ever since. Clement of Alexandria,[5] and Gregory of Nazianzen, as well as the "heretic" Heracleon, quoted from the *Preaching of Peter*.[6] And Origen, when he mentions the book, does not venture to pronounce absolutely on its character.[6] The *Shepherd of Hermas*, a book in high repute in the early church, and one which distinctly claims to have been inspired,[7] was quoted by Irenæus as "Scripture."[8] Clement of Alexandria said it was a divine revelation;[9] and Origen said it was divinely inspired,[10] and quoted it as "Holy Scripture" at the same time that he cited the Psalms and the Epistles of Paul;[11] and Athanasius quotes it.[12] Dionysius of Alexandria cites the *Wisdom of Jesus, the Son of Sirach*, as "divine;"[13] Hilary of Poitiers quotes it with the words, "Do they hear the Lord?"[14] Athanasius cites it as the saying of the Holy Spirit,[15] and as Scripture.[16] Ephrem called it Scripture;[17] Jerome quoted it as "Divine Scripture."[18] Origen quotes the *Wisdom of Solomon* as the "Word of God,"[19] and the "words of Christ himself."[20] Cyprian

---

1 Davidson, Canon, 117 (91).
2 Strom., iii. 9 (M 1724, ii. 113).
3 Ch. iv. (M 1721, p. 105).
4 De Habitu Muliebri, ch. 3, (M 1730, vol. 1, p. 307).
5 Strom., vi. 5 (M 1724, ii. 326); vi. 15 (Ibid., p. 379).
6 Westcott, Canon, 302 (276).
7 Westcott, Canon, 194 (177).
8 Adv. Hær., iv. 20, 2 (M 1593, p. 364).
9 Strom., i. 29 (M 1724, vol. 1, p. 469).
10 Comm. in Ep. ad Rom, xvi. 14.
11 De Prin. iii. 2, § 4 (M 1729, i. 230).
12 Contra Arianos, ii. iv. (M 1575, i. 7).
13 De Natura, 3 (M 1735, p. 178).
14 Ex. Op. Hist. Fragmentum, iii.
15 Davidson, Canon, 177.
16 Letter to the Bishops of Egypt and Libya, § 5 (M 1577, p. 128).
17 Davidson, Canon, 204.
18 Ibid., 191.
19 Contra Cels., iii. 72 (M 1729, ii. 150).
20 In Lucam Hom., 21.

ascribes it to the "Holy Spirit,"[1] and calls it "Divine Scripture."[2]
Eusebius of Cæsarea cites it as a "Divine Oracle;"[3] Ephrem quotes it;[4]
St. Chrysostom used it as Scripture.[5]   Eusebius of Cæsarea quotes
Daniel xiii. as Scripture;[6] so does Ephrem.[7]   Daniel has not a thirteenth
chapter now.   The church has since taken it away.   Lucifer of Cag-
liari (370 A. D.) quoted *First Maccabees* as "Holy Scripture;"[8]   Athanasius quotes the first book of *Esdras;*[9] Clement of Alexandria called
the writer of the fourth book of *Esdras* a prophet;[10] he thought *Baruch*
as much the word of God as any other book, and he quotes it as
Divine Scripture.[11]   Alexander of Thessalonica calls it Holy Scripture;[12] Cyril of Jerusalem calls its writer a prophet.[13]   Cyril is one
of those who said, "Thou must hate all heretics."[14]   Clement of
Alexandria cites Barnabas as an apostle.[15]   So he cites the Roman
Clement.[16]   Origen quotes from the *Epistle of Barnabas,*[17] calls it
"Holy Scripture," and places it on a level with the Psalms and
the Epistles of Paul.[18]   As late as the fourth century many good
Christians assigned to the *Epistle of Barnabas* and the *Pastor of Hermas*
as much authority as Christians do to the books now called inspired.[19]
Cyprian cites *Tobit* as "Holy Scripture."[20]   Clement of Alexandria

1 Exhor. Martyr., ch. 12 (M 1728, ll. 74).

2 Ep. ad Serg., Rog. 1 (M 1588, ll. 13).   3 Præpar. Evan., l. 9.

4 Davidson, Canon, 204.   5 Expos. in Ps. clx. 7.   In Gen. xl. 1.

6 Demon. Evang., vi. 19.   7 Davidson, Canon, 204.   8 Ibid., 194.

9 Contra Arianos, II. xvi. 3 (M 1575, ll. 309).   10 Strom., iii. 16 (M 1724, ll. 132).

11 Pæd., ll. 3 (M 1724, l. 212).   12 Epis. ad Athanasium (M 1577, p. 95).

13 Catech., xi. 15 (M 1589, p. 117).   14 Catech., vi. 20 (M 1589, p. 70).

15 Strom., ll. 6 (M 1724, ll. 19); ll. 20, (p. 66).   16 Ibid., iv. 17 (p. 187).

17 Contra Cels., l. 63 (M 1729, l. 468).

18 De Prin., iii. 2, § 4 (M 1729, l. 230, 231, top of page).

19 "When Were Our Gospels Written?" Tischendorf; Religious Tract Society's
authorized edition, London, 1869, p. 30 (M 102).

20 "On the Lord's Prayer," § 32 (M 1728, l. 419).

also calls it Scripture,[1] and he wrote comments on the *Epistle of Barnabas* and the *Revelation of Peter.*[2]

These are merely a few of the instances in which the early Fathers cited as divine and inspired, books no longer considered so, but they illustrate the fact that in the primitive days there were books in the Bible which are no longer there. Some of them have indeed been retained by the Catholic church and rejected by the Protestant, but many have been rejected by both.

And not only did the early Christian writers in quoting their authorities not limit themselves to the books which are in our Bible to-day, but the New Testament writers did not confine themselves to canonical books. When Paul commanded " to remember the words of the Lord Jesus, how he said, 'It is more blessed to give than to receive,'"[3] he quoted either from tradition or from some apocryphal work. There is no such saying in the Four Gospels. In 1 Cor. ii. ·9, a passage is quoted as scripture which is not in the Old Testament, but which both Origen and Jerome say was taken from an apocryphal work, *The Revelation of Elias.*[4] In Acts, xvii. 28, Paul quotes *verbatim et literatim* from the *Phenomena* of the Greek poet Aratus and from the *Hymn to Jupiter* of Cleanthes.[5] The famous saying "Evil communications corrupt good manners," in 1 Cor. xv. 33, was quoted by Paul from the Thaïs of Menander, one of the seven wise men of Greece.[6] And, in Titus, i. 12, the writer quotes from the Greek poet

1 Strom., 11. 23 (M 1724, 11. 79).
2 Euseb. Eccl. Hist., vi. 14 (219) ; Westcott, Canon, p. 512 (484).
3 Acts, xx. 35.
4 Origen Tract. xxxv., § 17 in Matt.; Jerome ad Isaiæ, lxiv., Epis. cl.
5 Clarke, comm. l. c. (M 118, iii. 841). 6 Ibid., l. c. (ibid., iv. 297).

Epimenides,[1] and calls him a prophet. Matthew says, "That it might be fulfilled which was spoken by the prophet, 'I will open my mouth in parables; I will utter things which have been kept secret.' "[2] There is no such prophecy in the Old Testament. The writer was quoting from some apocryphal book. And Jude makes quotations from the apocryphal books of Enoch[3] and *The Ascension of Moses*.[4]

Moreover, many of these books were in early days read in the Sabbath services in churches even from the apostolic age,[5] exactly as Matthew, Mark, Luke and John are now. The *Gospel of Peter* was in use in the church at Rhossus as well as in other early churches.[6] The *Revelation of Peter* and the *Revelation of Paul* were read in the churches of Palestine, the home of Jesus, so late as 390 A. D.[7] The *Epistle of Clement* to the Corinthians was in use from the earliest times,[8] and continued so even in Jerome's day in the fifth century.[9] Eusebius says that both before and in his time it was read in most of the churches;[10] and it stands to this day among the canonical books in the Alexandrine manuscript,[11] and in the Apostolic Canon.[12] He also says that the *Shepherd of Hermas* was used in the churches,[13] and we know that a translation of it was found in a

---

[1] Clarke, Comm., l. c. (M 118, iv. 668).   [2] Matt. xiii. 35.

[3] Jude, 14.   [4] Ibid., 9; cf. Origen, de Prin., III., ii. 1 (M 1729, i. 222). The disappearance of the title of this apocryphal work from the text of the book of Jude is of the same character as the disappearance of the word Isaiah from Mark, i. 2, as mentioned in note 13 on page 61.

[5] Westcott, Canon, 1 6 (169), 204 (187).

[6] Euseb. Eccl. Hist., vi. 12 (217).

[7] Sozomen, Eccl. Hist., vii. 19 (1 324, p. 344).

[8] Euseb. Eccl. Hist., iv. 23 (149); iii. 16 (90); Epiph. Hær., xxx. 15.

[9] Jerome, De Vir. Ill. 15.   [10] Eccl. Hist., iii. 16 (90).

[11] Westcott, Canon, 545 (515).   [12] Apost. Const., VIII., xlvii. 85 (M 1753, p. 269).

[13] Euseb. Eccl. Hist., iii. 3 (72).

manuscript of the Latin Bible so late as the fifteenth century,[1] only four centuries ago.

Eusebius, in the place just referred to, where he says that the *Shepherd of Hermas* was read in the churches, mentions indeed the fact that it was disputed by some; but he says the same thing of the Epistles of James and Jude—that while they were considered spurious, they were still read in the churches.[2] No orthodox theologian dare say to-day that the Epistle of James is spurious, even if he believed it to be so. And yet the only difference between the books is, that while the three started on precisely the same footing, James and Jude found their way into the Bible, while the *Shepherd of Hermas* was kept out. Theodoret found more than two hundred copies of Tatian's *Diatessaron* in use in the churches of Syria, and he removed them, and put the Four Gospels in their place.[3] He also found the *Gospel according to the Hebrews* in circulation.[3] *The Gospel of Nicodemus* had a place in the cathedral of Canterbury, in England, so late as the seventeenth century,[4] less than two centuries ago. People think that the Bible has always been just what it is now, and that because all is serene and calm now, it has ever been so. Nothing could be further from the truth. The New Testament has been different in different ages.

The reader should bear in mind that these references are to the early Christian Fathers, who saw much of what they wrote, who heard these books read in the churches, and who in many instances themselves read them.

---

[1] Westcott, Canon, 9 (9).   [2] Eccl. Hist., II. 23 (67).
[3] Theod. Hæret. Fab., I. 20.   [4] Westcott, Canon, 337 (359).

The idea of a New Testament, such as we now have, was not entertained then. It was the product of centuries later. In the early days it was somewhat as now with the text books used in colleges. Chicago University may have one series of mathematics, Michigan University another, and Harvard University still another; but no one of these institutions pretends that it has all the text books on mathematics worth anything, or that its books contain all the truth and the others all falsehood. For its particular use each college prefers a certain series, and that series it adopts. So one Father could accept books which another would reject, and reject books which another would adopt, and the contents of the Bible depended on the opinions of the Father. He accepted only those books which taught his preconceived ideas. As has been already observed, the Bible did not form the beliefs; the beliefs formed the Bible.

CHAPTER VII.

THE HERETICS.

But one answer has ever been made to these facts, and that is that they were the result of heresy. The orthodox theologians of this age assume to be the inheritors of pure and unadulterated Christianity, as taught by the orthodox Fathers of the early ages, and they say that while the New Testament, as we now have it, was recognized by the Fathers, the extra-canonical books were used and the intra-canonical books were discarded solely by the heretics. Very intelligent men make this claim, and the wonder is that it should have to be discussed. I need hardly say to the reader that the theory is quite groundless. We have seen in a preceding chapter that the orthodox Fathers declared many books to be divine and inspired which are now without the canon, and are declared by orthodox theologians of to-day to be uninspired; and we shall see in the next chapter that, on the other hand, many orthodox Fathers' rejected books which are to-day in the canon and considered the word of God. Irenæus denied the Pauline authorship of the Epistle to the Hebrews [1], yet no one calls him a heretic. In fact, he wrote a book against heresies himself. Hippolytus also denied its Pauline authorship,[2] and he, too, wrote a book "Against All Heresies." Heresy was an easy charge in those days. Tertullian, one of the founders of the New Testament, became a Montanist[3]—that

1 Westcott, Canon, 330, (352).   2 Ibid., 376 (348).   3 Ibid., 367 (339).

is, one of a sect which simply proposed to restore Christianity[1]—
and that made him a heretic.[2]   And he, too, wrote a work against
heretics.   Justin wrote against the heretics, Epiphanius did the same
thing, and so did Theodoret.   Every man in that age called every
other man a heretic who did not think as he did.   This is the "simplicity of primitive Christianity."   The early believers convicted one
another of heresy on the authority of disputed books, almost before
the books themselves had become a part of the Bible.[3]   St. Cyprian
implicitly denied that Hebrews was written by Paul,[4] and, generally
speaking, no Latin Father previous to Hilary (368 A. D.) admits that
it was written by him.[5]   But nobody now calls them heretics.   If it
were not written by Paul we should say that those persons were
worthy of honor who opposed its introduction to the Bible; and that
is what the heretics did.[6]   Dionysius (231 A. D.), the pupil of
Origen, did not believe Revelation was written by the Apostle John.[7]
No one calls him a heretic, but if he lived in this age, and said so, he
would be thus denominated.   Towards the beginning of the third
century, Hebrews, 2 Peter, James, Jude, 2 John, 3 John and Revelation,
all of which are in the Bible to-day, were only partly received by the
orthodox writers;[8] even so late as the fourth century there is no trace
in the Latin churches of the use of the Epistles of James or 2 Peter;[9]
and in the Greek Syrian churches, at the beginning of the fourth
century, there are only traces of a complete canon.[10]   Yet no one calls

---

1 Ibid., 396 (368).   2 Ibid., 383 (355).
3 This was the case with Arius. See Westcott, Canon, 425 (397).
4 Westcott, 368 (340, top line).   5 Ibid., 369, (340).   6 Davidson, Canon, 237.
7 Euseb. Eccl. Hist., vii. 25 (282).   8 Westcott, Canon, 325 (297), 394 (305-6).
9 Ibid., 392 (364).   10 Ibid., 391 (363).

those people heretical. The orthodox writers did the same thing which the heretics are now charged with doing; and books have been received as authoritative and even of divine authority by evangelical teachers who denied or doubted their apostolic authorship.[1]

Neither is it true, as has sometimes been claimed, that the heretics were the authors of all the forgeries and corruptions, while the orthodox people were innocent. The latter said, it is true, that the former had perpetrated the forgeries,[2] but the former also said it was the latter who had done so;[3] and while the orthodox ecclesiastics charged the heretics with mutilating or corrupting the Scriptures,[4] the charge can not always be maintained,[5] and the orthodox Christians did the same thing.[6] Prof. Davidson, the author whom I am quoting so frequently, proposed, and not without good reason, to change the text of the Bible so as to remove the contradictions which modern unbelievers have used so powerfully against orthodoxy. He says:

"It is time that the text of these historical books should be rectified in those instances where an unquestionable necessity exists. If there be not manuscript evidence to warrant certain changes, we should not be deterred from making them. Common sense, the credit of the inspired writers, and, above all, their sacred authority, outweigh all scruples about correcting by *conjecture*. *Real*

---

1 Ibid., 364 (396). Calvin did so, as will be seen later.
2 Westcott 275 (254); Iren., C. Hær., iii. xi. 9 (M 1725, vol. 1, p. 296); ibid., i. xx. 1 (p. 79).
3 Const. Apost., vi. 16, ff. (M 1753, p. 159).
4 Tertull. de Præscr. Hær., 30 (M 1730, ii. 35); Orig. Contra Cels., ii. 27 (M 1729, ii. 33).
5 Westcott, 311 (284).
6 Davidson, Intro. N. T., ii., 516 (M 104); Westcott, Canon, 398 (360); also the second reference in note 17 supra.

contradictions should never be allowed to tarnish a text written under the immediate supervision of the Holy Spirit."[1]

Dr. Adam Clarke, the venerable Methodist commentator, proposed the same thing;[2] and we have a very marked instance of the change of text by orthodox scholars in the recent revision. They made the revision to correct the text. So did the heretics; and they said they were correcting, and not corrupting it.[3] They acted in good faith, and orthodoxy now impugns their motives while doing the same thing. It is a strange mental trait which permits an action to be entirely right in our sect, and entirely wrong in another's. No opprobrium should be attached to those early Christians simply on the charge of heresy. "Heretic" does not mean a bad or a depraved man, nor a man who believes what is not true. It means a man who uses his own judgment in selecting his belief, rather than submits his judgment to another. The church, to maintain its power, has undertaken the control of belief, and has prescribed what it should be, and the heretic has been the man whose opinion differed from the church's. In very many instances the heretic has been right and the church has been wrong, in many cases it has been the reverse, and in many more both have been wrong. But the principle at stake has been, and ever must be, that a man has the right to do his own thinking. To be called by epithets has ever been the penalty which intelligence pays to ignorance; and to suffer, the tribute which genius pays to mediocrity. The man who uses the word heretic but betrays his intellectual debasement, and, as between two men, one

---

[1] Kitto's Cyclopedia of Biblical Literature, Art. Chronicles, under the head "Discrepancies and Contradictions." The italics are his.

[2] Comm. on 1 Sam., xvii. 58 (M 118, i. 711).   [3] Euseb. Eccl. Hist., v. 28 (208).

orthodox and the other heterodox or heretical, the latter is always the more intelligent and almost invariably the more noble and the more moral. So it was with the early heretics. Carpocrates, one of them, taught that men were to be saved by faith and love.[1] Cerinthus, another, believed that after the resurrection Jesus was to establish an earthly kingdom[2]—a doctrine which has since become one of the commonest orthodox beliefs. Yet for this, it is said, John, "the beloved disciple," would not remain in the same house with him.[3] The most famous of the so-called heretics was Marcion, who flourished about the middle of the second century. His offense consisted solely of being a follower of Paul as opposed to the Petrines. He seems to have been a high-minded and excellent man, notwithstanding the efforts of his enemies to defame his character. What he desired was, to reproduce, in its original simplicity, the Gospel of St. Paul,[4] and for this, Polycarp, whose orthodoxy is unquestioned, called him the "first born of Satan."[5] He said that he wished to introduce no innovation, but only to restore what had been corrupted.[4] He had rationalistic tendencies,[6] and he wanted a stricter discipline and a sterner logic in the church.[7] He aimed to establish a new line of bishops,[8] with St. Paul at its head, and, as the Petrine line was already established, this was what modern politics calls an "unholy alliance," striking at the bread and butter of the men already in, and hence the efforts to blacken his character.

[1] Irenæus, Adv. Hær., I. 25, 5 (M 1593, p. 77).
[2] Euseb. Eccl. Hist., III., 28 (102).
[3] Iren. Adv. Hær., III. 3, 4 (M 1725, I. 263); Euseb. Eccl. Hist., III. 28 (103).
[4] Tert. Adv. Marc., I. 20 (M 1727, p. 35).   [5] Iren. Adv. Hær., III. 3, 4 (M 1725, I. 263)
[6] Westcott, Canon, 393 (365).   [7] Ibid., 315 (287.)
[8] Ibid., 312 (285).

It is not true, therefore, that the heretics were responsible for all the theological vagaries, or were worse than orthodox Christians. They were quite as good, and quite as well educated. Moreover, why they should now be called heretics is a mystery, since they were the originators of the most vital of the accepted beliefs of to-day. Putting the unorthodox sects into one group, and calling them heretics, and the orthodox sects into another, we find that the heretics have used nearly all the books now called canonical.[1] They revered them as much as the orthodox sects did.[2] They appealed to the New Testament to support their views.[3] *They were the first to call it scriptural and inspired, and to place it on a level with the Old Testament.*[4] They were the real originators of the belief that the New Testament is the word of God. The Christian Fathers subsequently caught the usefulness of the idea, and introduced it into "orthodox" Christianity. Now it is the heretic who says the New Testament is not inspired, but in the early days it was the heretic who said it was. Moreover, their idea of inspiration was as complete as that of Origen himself.[5] They were the first to form a canon;[6] and the first to write commentaries on the Gospels.[7] The first canonical list ever adopted was by a council in which the majority were heretics,[8] and this same list was subsequently ratified by the orthodox Council of Constantinople in 692 A. D.,[9] and again by the equally ortho-

---

[1] Westcott, Canon, 269 (248), 280 (259), 299 (273).   [2] Ibid., 285 (262), 291 (265).

[3] Iren. Adv. Hær., iii. 11, 7 (M 1593, p. 234); Tertull. de Præscr. Hær., 14 (M 1730, ii. 19); Westcott, Canon, 302 (275).

[4] Westcott, 289 (263), 308 note 2 (282, note 1).   [5] Ibid., 301 (274).

[6] Ibid., 308 (282); Davidson, Canon, 110 (86).   [7] Westcott, Canon, 302 (275).

[8] Davidson, 173 (135); Westcott, 433 (405, bottom line).

[9] Westcott, 434 (405).

dox Council of Aix-la-Chapelle,[1] and it had a wide circulation in the Isidorian version of the canons.[1] The heretics, equally with the orthodox people, recognized the Scriptures as the common ground on which questions at issue were to be settled.[2] Our present Gospel of John originated with the heretics, but it was not by them assigned to the apostle.[3] It was the orthodox Christians who subsequently took it and forged John's name to it.[3] In fact, since much of what we now call orthodoxy was obtained from these people, modern theologians show little gratitude in echoing the maledictions of the early ecclesiastics in calling them heretics. It is quite time that Christian scholars ceased to bow so abjectly before the authority of ignorant Fathers, whose opinions were not so valuable as their own.

I should not have given so much space to this part of the subject, were it not that theologians try to show that the New Testament, as we now have it, has always been in use in the orthodox church, and that everything else is due to the heretics. The theory is quite baseless.

1 Ibid., 435 (406-7).   2 Ibid., 395 (367).
3 Davidson, Intro. N. T., 11, 520, § 2 (M 104).

CHAPTER VIII.

THE CHRISTIAN CANON.

We now come to the formation of the Christian canon—to the process by which it was evolved.   In a preceding chapter I gave a brief outline of the formation of the Old Testament canon among the Hebrews, and left the Old Testament canon among the Christians to be detailed with the New Testament, preferring to give them together, and thus preserve the unity.   Beginning with the first two centuries of the Christian Church, we find that there was no New Testament as we now understand that term.   More than forty Gospels and a much greater number of Acts, Epistles and Revelations were in use.   The writer of the Gospel according to Luke says, "Forasmuch as many have taken in hand to set forth in order a declaration of these things," etc., showing that when he wrote many Gospels were already in existence.   From the mass of writings then in circulation the books in our New Testament were taken, and the other books dropped out of use.[1]   Origen says:

"And that not four Gospels, but very many were written, out of which these we have were chosen and delivered to the churches, we may perceive."[2]

The selection of the books, and the formation of the list, were a very slow process, and it is "impossible to point to any period as marking the date at which our present canon was determined."[3]

---

[1] Westcott, Canon, 183 (167).
[3] Westcott, Canon, 496 (468).

[2] In Prœm. Luc., hom. 1, vol. 3, p. 210.

"This result [the formation of the canon] was obtained gradually, spontaneously, silently. There is no evidence to show that at any time the claims of the apostolic writings to be placed on an equal footing with the Old Testament, which formed the first Christian Bible, were deliberately discussed and admitted. . . . . Step by step the books which were stamped with apostolic authority were separated from the mass of other works which contained the traditions of less authoritative teachers."[1]

When the Catholic Church began to be formed, about the year 170–180 A. D., the tendency was to use fewer books, and the ones accepted as authoritative began to be called divine. The reader will observe that I have said in one place that the early Fathers originated the theory that these books were divinely inspired, and in another place that the heretics did so. There is no contradiction here. Both the Fathers and the heretics were Christians—they simply belonged to different sects. In the contest for the mastery it so happened that the sects to which the Fathers belonged—the Petrine—gained the supremacy, and from them arose the present Christian Church. Had the other sects gained the victory, their Fathers would now be the orthodox authorities and the others would be the heretics. Now, it is true that in the so-called heretical sects originated the theory that the New Testament was divine and of equal authority with the Old, but that doctrine would not have been accepted by us had not the orthodox Fathers of that time adopted it into their sects. We are the descendants of the orthodox sects, and so far as we are concerned the early Fathers originated the theory. They did it to have authority for the new and unusual doctrines coming into use, just as the heretics were using the same theory to support their

1 Westcott, Canon, 345 (317) ff.
6

doctrines. The books were, in those days, mainly in the hands of
the bishops.[1]   The laity had nothing to do with them. Not one in
ten thousand of the laity could read.   The recognition of the authority of the New Testament was brought about entirely by ecclesiastical usage.[2]   Each Father included in the newly forming Bible
what books he liked, and excluded what he did not like.   The consequence was, there were as many Bibles in those days as there were
Fathers engaged in making them.   In their differences of opinion as
to what constituted the canon, the Fathers made no attempt to compare the books by a critical investigation into the history of the
records themselves.[3] Dr. Westcott says the canon was "formed by
instinct and not by argument."[4]   Instinct is not a good thing to
form a Bible by.   The Fathers contended for centuries as to what
should go into the list until they found they could not agree, and
then the church held councils and voted on it, and the books which
polled the most votes went in.   St. Augustine was a great advocate
of this plan.   He thought that the books which were received by all
the churches should be in the Bible; and that in the case of books
on which there was a difference of opinion, the majority voice of the
churches should decide it.[5]   An exact parallel to this is found in the
manner of making changes in the recent New Testament revision.
On the first reading of a disputed text a majority vote authorized the
amendment, but on the second and final reading a two-thirds vote o
all those present was necessary.[6]   But even this plan did not work
satisfactorily in the church, for the councils differed.   One counc

1 Davidson, 164 (128).   2 Westcott, Canon, 185 (165); Ibid., 12 (12).
3 Ibid., 408 (375).   4 Ibid., 368 (335).   5 De Doct. Christ., ii. 8 (M 1742, p. 41).
6 Revised New Testament, Preface, II., fifth rule of May 25, 1870.

would adopt a list inserting books which another had rejected, and rejecting books which another had inserted, and this continued until the church held one great council, adopted a final list, and said: "This is the Bible. Believe it or be damned." Let us now go over the history of the past two thousand years, and see what have been the fluctuations and the variations in the canon.

The first collection of New Testament books ever made was by Marcion,[1] the "heretic," about the year 145 A. D. It consisted of one Gospel and ten of Paul's Epistles;[2] and they were not then considered the word of God.

"Faith in the divine authority or inspiration of current books had not yet arisen. . . . [Marcion] did not consider Paul's Epistles inspired or of divine authority."[3]

This was more than seventy-five years after Paul was dead. The Epistles which Marcion accepted were Galatians, First and Second Corinthians, Romans, First and Second Thessalonians, Ephesians, Colossians, Philippians and Philemon.[3] He omitted First and Second Timothy, Titus and Hebrews, which we have since called genuine and placed in the Bible. His Gospel has been the subject of much controversy, the orthodox people asserting that it was Luke's mutilated; and the unbelievers denying this, and asserting that it was the manuscript from which Luke's Gospel was subsequently made up. The facts are these: Marcion's Gospel had no name.[4] Indeed, as St. Chrysostom observes, none of the

---

1 Westcott, 808 (282).　　　2 Tertullian, Adv. Marc., v. (M 1727, p. 368 ff.) ,
3 Davidson, Intro. N. T., ii. 516-7 (M 104, vol. 2),
4 Tert., Adv. Hær., iv. 2 (M 1727, p. 180).

apostles affixed their signatures to the Gospels now bearing their
names.[1] That was the work of the church long afterward, and
we have simply the church's word that they are genuine. And
thus we find that in Marcion's time, more than a century after
Jesus was dead, even if a Gospel by Luke were in existence, his
name had not yet been attached to it. If Marcion's were Luke's
Gospel the question arises, How does it happen that a heretic was
in possession of a genuine Gospel before the church itself was?
and was his heresy anything more than in the name? Marcion's
Gospel was identical, word for word, with about three-fourths of
the present Gospel of Luke, and it was shorter than Luke. Now,
the reader knows how annotations made on the margin of a manuscript find their way into the text in the process of copying, and
thus in time increase the length of a work, so that of two manuscripts
of the same book, one shorter than the other, the shorter is generally
the older. As I have said, Marcion's Gospel was the shorter. The
charge has been made that Marcion purposely mutilated Paul's
Epistles and Luke's Gospel to suit his doctrinal needs. It originated with Irenæus, and was repeated with great violence by Tertullian and Epiphanius, and has been reiterated by theologians ever
since, until very recently orthodoxy itself begins to admit that it is
not true.[2] So far from Marcion being a "heretic," he included in
his canonical list all that he considered to be the genuine Christian
books,[3] and he gives indications of having been a much more care-
ful scholar than his accusers. The Epistle which we now call "to

---

[1] Hom. 1. in Epis. ad Rom. (M 1590, p. 6).
[2] Westcott, 311 (284).   [3] Davidson, Intro. N. T., ii. 517 (M 104, vol. 2).

the Ephesians " he called " to the Laodiceans," and he prided himself on having restored its true name.[1] He omitted from his Gospel the parable of the prodigal son,[2] and from the Epistle to the Romans the last two chapters,[3] either because they were not there in his time, or because he was satisfied they were interpolations. Some illustrations of the charges against him will indicate their worthless character. Tertullian says that he eliminated from Luke's Gospel the saying of Jesus that he came not to destroy the law and the prophets, but to fulfil.[4] That passage is not in Luke, but in Matthew,[5] yet Tertullian actually repeats this charge on three subsequent occasions.[6] He says that Marcion must expunge "I am not sent but unto the lost sheep of the house of Israel," and "It is not meet to take the children's bread, and give it to the dogs."[7] They also are not in Luke, but in Matthew.[8] Epiphanius likewise charges him with having omitted a passage which in reality is in Matthew and not in Luke.[9] The charge that he mutilated the canonical list, and those books which he accepted, will not stand. There is another noteworthy thing: No writer before Marcion's time makes mention of the Gospel according to Luke, and no writer after him does so till Irenæus, nearly fifty years later. These are the facts. Many think they are sufficient to give ground for suspicion that some one afterwards took Marcion's Gospel and forged Luke's name to it. Others do not. The reader can decide for himself.

---

1 Tert., Adv. Marc., v. 17 (M 1727, p. 456).   2 Westcott, 312 (285), note 1.
3 Origen, Comm. in Rom., xvi. 25.   4 Adv. Marc., iv. 7 (M 1727, p. 192).
5 Matt., v. 17.   6 Adv. Marc., iv. 9 (p. 204), iv. 12 (p. 220), iv. 36 (333).
7 Ibid., iv. 7 (M. 1727, p. 192).
8 Matt., xv. 24, 26.   9 Hær., xlii

The first Old Testament list by a Christian writer, was by Melito, bishop of Sardis, about 175 A. D.   He wrote to Onesimus:

"As you . . . were desirous of having an exact statement of the Old Testament, how many in number, and in what order the books were written, I have endeavored to perform this. . . .   When, therefore, I went to the East and came as far as the place where these things were proclaimed and done, I accurately ascertained the books of the Old Testament, and send them to thee here below. The names are as follows: Of Moses, five books, Genesis, Exodus, Leviticus, Numbers, Deuteronomy; Joshua, Judges, Ruth; four of Kings, (1 Samuel, 2 Samuel, 1 Kings, 2 Kings), two of Chronicles, the Psalms of David; Proverbs of Solomon, which is also called Wisdom, Ecclesiastes, Song of Songs, Job; of Prophets, Isaiah, Jeremiah; of the twelve prophets, one book; Daniel, Ezekiel, Ezra, Nehemiah."[1]

There are three things to which I wish to call the reader's attention:

1. So late as the year 175 A. D., a bishop in the Christian Church could not say what books were in the Old Testament till he had traveled in the East and made inquiries.

2. In giving the list "accurately," he omits Esther and Lamentations.

3. He was so little versed in the sacred writings that he did not know that Proverbs and the Wisdom of Solomon were two entirely different books.

Irenæus was the real founder of the New Testament canon.   His date is from 180 to 200 A. D.   Of our Gospels Luke was probably compiled or written about 170 A. D., Mark about 175 A. D., John about 178 A. D., and Matthew about 180 A. D.   Irenæus began to

---

1 Eusebius, Eccl. Hist., iv. 26 (152).

use them within a very short time after their origin, though it was probably not till the year 200 A. D. that he knew of them all. He used them exclusively, and his canon consisted of the Four Gospels, Acts, thirteen Epistles of Paul, (rejecting Hebrews), First John, and Revelation.[1] In an appendix he placed, Prof. Davidson thinks, as of less authority, Second John, First Peter and the *Shepherd of Hermas.*[1] The Epistle to the Hebrews, Jude, James, Second Peter and Third John he ignored.[1] As the reader sees, this is the first time we meet with anything like a recognition of our present canon; and Irenæus rejected several books which we now call divine. As he is the earliest writer to mention the Four Gospels, orthodox theologians now assert that they must have been in use before, and recognized as sources of authority; because, they say, it would not have been possible—if, as unbelievers assert, other Gospels had been in use before—to discard those others and to substitute a new series in their places. The reply to this is, that it was not only possible, but it is what occurred, as history testifies. The intense rivalry between the different sects in the first two centuries, and especially between the Paulines, the Petrines and the Johannines, had taught them that neither could master the other, and neither could hold exclusively to its special books, and insist on their adoption. The result was a compromise, just as in a presidential convention, when the friends of the leading candidates find that neither of the favorites can be nominated, they unite on an entirely new man, one who before has hardly been mentioned. The Catholic Church was just forming (about 170 A. D.), by the union of the small sects and

1 Davidson, Canon, 123 (163).

churches into one great body, and the necessity of some written source of authority, of a Bible recognized by all, was apparent; and it was this need which formed the canon ¹ The old books were discarded or suppressed, and the new ones took their place. Previously no two sects had used entirely the same books, and many used only one; and this was true even for a long time after our Four Gospels came into use, and after the effort was made to form one universal canon. Thus the Ebionites² and the Cerinthians³ used only St. Matthew; the Cerdonians only Marcion's Gospel.⁴ The Marcionites used, of course, only their own Gospel. The Theodotians rejected St. John, as did also the Alogi;⁵ and the Petrine Christians naturally preferred Mark's Gospel, which was Petrine,⁶ just as the Paulists preferred Luke, which favored Paul.⁶ In the midst of these facts church strength could come only in union and in the adoption of books which should be acceptable to all. That the Bible is such a compromise, its contents attest. The Gospel according to Matthew is Petrine, it being there that Jesus is represented as saying to Peter, "Upon this rock will I build my church."⁷ Mark is also Petrine, and Luke is Pauline, as the early Christian Fathers testify.⁶ The Epistles of Peter are Petrine, the Epistles of Paul are Pauline, and the Gospel according to John, the Epistles of John, and Revelation, are, of course, Johannine. I have said that history records at this time the suppression of the old Gospels and the substitution of the new. Thus, Serapion, Bishop of Antioch,

---

¹ Davidson, Canon, 134 (105), 136 (106). 144, 164 (128).
² Iren , Adv. Hær., 1. 26, § 2, III. 11, § 7.   ³ Epiph IIær., xxviii. 5; xxx. 3, 14.
⁴ Pseudo-Tert , Adv. Om. Hær., vi. (M 1730, vol. 3, p. 269).
⁵ Blunt, "Dictionary of Sects," Alogi.
⁶ Tert., Adv. Marc., iv. 5 (M 1727, p. 187).   ⁷ Matt., xvi. 18.

(190 A. D.), while on a visit to the church of Rhossus, in Cilicia, found them using the *Gospel of Peter*. Being appealed to, he per-mitted them to read it, notwithstanding the controversies it produced. Later he wrote, "But when I came to you I had supposed that all held to the true faith; and as I had not perused the Gospel presented by them under the name of Peter, I said, 'If this be the only thing that creates difference among you, let it be read.' But now having understood, from what was said to me, that their minds were enveloped in some heresy, I will make haste to come to you again."[1] Eusebius has preserved this extract, and though he does not say in so many words that the Gospel was suppressed, he intimates it, and it is conceded by eminent writers that that was done.[2] Again, early in the fifth century there was a man named Theodoret who was actively engaged in superintending the establishment of churches. In his travels he found the *Diatessaron*, or *Gospel of Tatian*, in use in orthodox churches, and he wrote:

"I found also myself more than two hundred such books in our churches which had been received with respect; and having gathered all together, I caused them to be laid aside, and introduced in their place the Gospels of the Four Evangelists."[3]

Dr. Westcott says that "from this statement it is clear that the Diatessaron was so orthodox as to enjoy a wide ecclesiastical popu-larity."[4]

The fact of displacement is also recognized by Prof Davidson:

[1] Euseb. Eccl. Hist., vi. 12 (217).
[2] Lost and Hostile Gospels, S. Baring Gould, p. 245 (M 445).
[3] Theod. Hæret. Fab., i. 20.   [4] Canon, 520 (291).

"Not until the latter half of the second century did the present Gospels assume a canonical position, *superseding other works of a similar character*, and receiving a divine authority."[1]

When, therefore, the orthodox clergy ask if it were possible that other Gospels could have been long in use in the early church and then have been suppressed and succeeded by our present Gospels, the reply is, That is exactly what occurred.

But why should there be just four Gospels? Why not five, or six, or a dozen? Irenæus, who was, as I have said, the real founder of the canon, and who spent his life in endeavoring to establish the Catholic Church and the Bible, determined this matter, and the church has followed him. Whatever reason he gives, therefore, for the present number of Gospels, will be the reason why we have that number. Fortunately, he is very explicit on this point, and we know exactly what decided him. He said that there were four quarters of the earth, and four universal winds, and that animals were four-legged, or four-formed, and therefore there should be four Gospels. His words are:

"It is not possible that the gospels can be either more or fewer in number than they are. For, since there are four quarters of the earth in which we live, and four universal winds, while the church is scattered throughout all the world, and the 'pillar and ground' of the church is the gospel and the spirit of life; it is fitting that she should have four pillars breathing out immortality on every side, and vivifying men afresh. . . . Therefore the gospels are in accord with these things. . . . For the living creatures are quadriform and the gospel is quadriform. . . . These things being so, all who destroy the form of the gospel are vain, unlearned, and also audacious; those (I mean) who represent the aspects

---

[1] 'ntrod. New Test., ii. 520 (M 104).

of the gospel as being either more in number than as aforesaid, or, on the other hand, fewer."[1]

I need not amuse the reader with the speculations of theologians endeavoring to discover every reason but the right one for the number of the Gospels. Indeed I might not amuse him, for it is a pitiful recital. There is no sadder spectacle in the intellectual world, than that of men possessed of really great mental possibilities, frittering away their time and their self-respect in trying to make a superstition appear reasonable by explaining its absurdities in an illogical manner, and, instead of walking erect in the dignity of a rational manhood, staggering along in a blind stupor, produced by the fumes of mysticism.

Those modern theologians who quote Irenæus as a learned and great man, do not take kindly to his argument for the number of the Gospels; nor to the fact that he said that the ministry of Jesus lasted twenty years,[2] and that Jesus was fifty years old when he was crucified.[3] And at the same time he was endeavoring to establish as of divine authority Gospels which said that Jesus' ministry lasted but three years!

The canon of Muratori,[3] the date of which is entirely unknown, but which orthodoxy places at the time of Irenæus, recognized the Four Gospels, Acts, thirteen Epistles of Paul, First John, Second John, Jude, and Revelation. It mentions the *Wisdom of Solomon*, which is no longer in the Bible, among the New Testament

[1] Adv. Hær., III., xi. 8 and 9. (M 1725, vol. 1, p. 293).

[2] Ibid., II. 22 (M 1725, II. 200 ff.)

[3] A Latin fragment of the canon found by Muratori in the Ambrosian library at Milan in 1740.

books; speaks approvingly of the *Shepherd of Hermas*, and says that
the Revelation of John and the *Revelation of Peter* were accepted
by the writer, although many were unwilling that the last should be
read in the churches.   It does not mention either First Peter, Second
Peter, First John, or James,[1] all of which are now in the Bible.
It speaks of the *Epistle to the Laodiceans*, calls the Epistle to
the Hebrews the *Epistle to the Alexandrians*,[2] and says both were
forgeries, passing under the name of Paul — a fact of which
modern theologians are discreetly silent, when they cite, as they do
with so much exultation, this manuscript as "early evidence of the
canon." The reader can judge of how desperately the church is in
need of support when, after a tremendous conflict, it is willing to
accept as "early evidence" a manuscript whose date is at least one
hundred and fifty years after Jesus Christ was dead.

Clement of Alexandria (210 A. D.) placed in his deutero-canon,
as having inferior authority, Hebrews, Second John, and Jude, which
are now in the Bible, and the *Revelation of Peter* (observe, not the
Revelation of John, but a different book), the *Shepherd of Hermas*,
the *First Epistle of Clement*, the *Second Epistle of Clement*, and the
Epistle of Barnabas,[3] which are not now in the Bible.   He thus
placed the Epistle to the Hebrews, Second John and Jude, which
are now in the Bible, on a level with the *Shepherd of Hermas* and
the *Epistle of Barnabas*, which are not in it.   He recognized no
distinct canon as of supreme authority,[4] and he did not attach our

---

[1] Westcott, Canon, 527 (498) ff.; (also translated, M 1725, il. 159).
[2] Davidson, Canon, 226.
[3] Ibid., 133 (109).   [4] Ibid., 139.

idea of "canonical" as opposed to "uncanonical" to either of the Four Gospels or to any other books of the New Testament.[1]

Tertullian (220 A. D.) included in his canon the Four Gospels, Acts, thirteen Epistles of Paul, First John, and Revelation;[2] he placed in an appendix, as not authoritative, Hebrews, Jude, Second John, and First Peter,[3] which are in the Bible now, and the *Shepherd of Hermas*, which is not; and he said nothing of James, Second Peter, and Third John,[3] which to-day are in the canon.

The Peshito, the Bible of the Ancient Syriac Christians, omitted Second Peter, Second John, Third John, Jude, and Revelation, all of which are now in our Bible.[3]

The old Latin version, the Bible of the early African Church, omitted the Epistle to the Hebrews, Second Peter, and James. The Epistle to the Hebrews was added subsequently as an anonymous book.[4]

The canon of the Abyssinian Church included, at first, Enoch, Fourth Esdras, the Ascension of Isaiah, the Jubilees, and Asseneth,[5] books which are not now in the Bible and of several of which the world now never hears. The list was changed frequently, and many books were eliminated or inserted, but, generally speaking, it contained Judith, Tobit, First Maccabees, Second Maccabees, Wisdom of Jesus, Wisdom of Solomon, and even a book called the Apocalypse of Isaiah,[5] none of which are now in our Bible.

The two canonical lists of upper and lower Egypt—called the

1 Ibid., 139.   2 Ibid., 139 (110).
3 Ibid., 146 (114); Westcott, Canon, 241 (221).
4 Westcott, 254 (234).   5 Davidson, Canon, 206 (162).

Thebaic version, or version of Thebes, and the Memphitic version, or the version of Memphis—omitted Revelation.[1]

Origen (250 A. D.) included in his Old Testament list the Epistle of Jeremiah, First Maccabees, and Second Maccabees, which are not in our Bible, and he makes no mention of Hosea, Joel, Amos, Obadiah, Jonah, Micah, Nahum, Habakkuk, Zephaniah, Haggai, Zechariah, and Malachi, which are in our Bible.[2]   The omission of these twelve books is very singular, and Rufinus' Latin version (400 A. D.) kindly inserts them.   Even if they were omitted by mistake, the error shows how careless and indifferent the Fathers were in stating what books were in the Bible.   Origen did not formulate a consecutive list of the New Testament books, but passages gathered here and there from his works indicate what his opinion was.[3]   He apparently divided them into three classes, authentic, unauthentic, and uncertain.   The first included the Four Gospels, Acts, fourteen Epistles of Paul, First Peter, First John, and the Revelation of John. The second included the *Shepherd of Hermas*—though he was rather inclined to place it in a higher class—the *Epistle of Barnabas*, the *Acts of Paul*, the *Gospel according to the Hebrews*, the *Gospel of the Egyptians*, and the *Preaching of Peter*.[4]   The third included the Epistles of James, Jude, Second Peter, Second John, and Third John,[4] all of which are in the Bible to-day.

Eusebius, the ecclesiastical historian, (340 A. D.), divided the books into three classes, the "acknowledged," the "disputed," and the "heretical."[5]   The "acknowledged" books included the Four

---

[1] Westcott, 366.   [2] Euseb. Eccl. Hist., vi. 25 (230).   [3] Ibid., (261).
[4] Davidson, Canon, 145 (114).   [5] Eccl. Hist., iii. 25 (99).

Gospels, the Acts, thirteen Epistles of Paul (omitting Hebrews), First John, and First Peter. They were the books concerning which there was no controversy. The "disputed" books he divided into two subordinate classes; the "generally known and recognized by most," namely, James, Jude, Second Peter, Second John, and Third John, none of which are disputed now, so far as the laity ever hears; and the "spurious," including the *Acts of Paul*, the *Shepherd of Hermas*, the *Revelation of Peter*, the *Epistle of Barnabas*, the *Teaching of the Apostles*, and the Revelation of John—which last is in the Bible to-day—and the *Gospel according to the Hebrews*. The "heretical" books included the *Gospel of Peter*, the *Gospel of Thomas*, the *Gospel of Matthew*, (not the one now in the Bible), the *Acts of the Apostles by Andrew*, and the *Acts of the Apostles by John*. The Epistle of James, which is now in the Bible and which he here classes as generally recognized, in another place he calls spurious;[1] and of Revelation he says that possibly it should be among the acknowledged books, but that some rejected it. The idea as to what composed the Bible was in the minds of the Fathers vague and indefinite. Such a strict and unalterable rule as we now have they did not possess. Eusebius was a bishop of the Eastern church, and the reader will observe as we progress that that church uniformly discarded Revelation.

Cyril, Bishop of Jerusalem, (356 A. D.), a member of the Eastern church, made a catalogue which included in the Old Testament Baruch, and the Epistle of Jeremiah, the Song of the Three Children, History of Susannah, and Bel and the Dragon, none of which are now in our Bible. His New Testament included the books now in it

1 Eccl. Hist., II. 23 (67).

except Revelation, and he adds, "But let all the rest be excluded.

And all the books which are not read in the churches, neither do thou read by thyself."[1]

The famous Gothic version of the Bible made by Ulphilas, a Gothic bishop, (360 A. D.), omitted the two books of Samuel and the books of Kings, because they contained accounts of wars likely to inflame the spirit of the Goths.[2] Only a small reason was needed in those days to keep a book out of the Bible.

More than three hundred and fifty years passed away, and it became apparent that the Fathers could not agree as to what books should be in the Bible, and councils began to deal with the matter. The first Christian assembly at which the canon was made the subject of a special ordinance was held at Laodicea in 365 A. D. Tertullian indeed mentions the fact that synods had acted upon the canonicity of books in his time,[3] but their authority must have been local and not general. Jerome also says that the council of Nicea included Judith in a list which it adopted,[4] but I can find no good evidence that the council of Nicea acted on the canon at all, although there is a very general impression that it did. Westcott thinks that it is only some casual reference which Jerome here alludes to. The current tradition is that the books were placed under a table at Nicea, and that after prayer the canonical ones leaped out from under, and the others remained behind. It is said that this story is told by Pappus, a Lutheran divine (1549—1601 A. D.) in his "Epitome

[1] Catech. Lect., iv. 35 (M 1589, p. 50).   [2] Westcott, Canon, 425 (397), note 4.
[3] De Pudic, 10 (M 1730, iii 83).
[4] Pref. in Judith, 1. p. 1169; Davidson, Canon, 171; Westcott, Canon, 426 (398), note 2.

Historiæ Ecclesiasticæ de Conversionibus Gentium," etc. It is, of course, fabulous, and probably originated from the fact that at the council of Chalcedon the Gospels were placed in the midst of the assembly.[1]

The synod of Laodicea was not a general council of the church, but its list was afterwards adopted by the church, so that virtually that was the first general action on the contents of the Bible. It was a gathering of twenty-four to thirty-two (the number is variously stated) of the clergy of Lydia and Phrygia. Whatever the number, the so-called heretics had a majority of the votes present.[2] Its decree was as follows:[3]

"Psalms composed by private men must not be read in the church, nor uncanonical books, but only the canonical books of the New and Old Testament. How many books must be read: "

Then follows the list[4] as we have it to-day, except that the Old Testament has Baruch and the Epistle of Jeremiah, neither of which are now in the Bible; and the New Testament omits Revelation. Observe for the first time the tone of authority as to what must and must not be read.

Athanasius, bishop of Alexandria, (365 A. D.), was at enmity with Eusebius and the clergy of Laodicea,[5] and when the latter declared that Revelation was not in the Bible, Athanasius immediately promulgated a list in which he declared that it was. In his canon he names, he says, the books in which alone were proclaimed the doctrine of godliness, and which no man must take from, and no

---

[1] Westcott, Canon, 426, (398), note 2.   [2] Davidson, 173 (135).
[3] Westcott, 429 (401).   [4] Its genuineness is doubtful.   [5] Davidson, Canon, 234.

7

man add to. Yet he omitted Esther, which the church has since
added, and he also inserted Baruch and the Letter of Jeremiah, which
the church has since taken away.[1] He expressly declared that Esther
was not a part of the Bible, and placed it on a level with the *Pastor
of Hermas*, and a book called *The Doctrine of the Apostles*. He closed
by saying, "Let there be no mention of apocryphal writings." He
had become tired of the controversy.

Amphilochius, Bishop of Iconium, (365 A. D.), also of the Eastern
church, omitted from the Old Testament Esther, but said that some
thought it should be included. In his New Testament he gives
the Four Gospels, Acts, and fourteen Epistles of Paul, and adds,
"But some maintain that the Epistle to the Hebrews is spurious;
not speaking well, for the grace (it shows) is genuine. To proceed:
What remains? Of the Catholic Epistles some maintain that we
ought to receive seven, and others three only, one of James, and
one of Peter, and one of John. . . . The Revelation of John
again some reckon among (the scriptures); but still *the majority say*
that it is spurious. This will be the most truthful canon of the
inspired scriptures."[2] The reader can not decide from that what he
considered "the most truthful canon," but it shows again how
entirely unsettled was the question as to what was the Bible and
what was not, and that the question was purely a matter of individual
opinion. His closing words show that in his time no list was universally accepted.

---

[1] Athanasius, Festal Epistle **XXXIX**, Library of the Fathers, Oxford, 1854; (M
1575, pp. 138, 139).

[2] Iambi ad Seleucum. Italics mine.

Gregory of Nazianzus, (389 A. D.), gave as the New Testament the Four Gospels, the Acts, fourteen Epistles of Paul, and the seven Catholic Epistles, and he adds, "In these you have all the inspired books; if there be any book besides these, it is not among the genuine (scriptures)."[1] He belonged to the Eastern church, and was thrusting at Revelation.

By the "seven Catholic Epistles" is meant always James, First Peter, Second Peter, First John, Second John, Third John, and Jude. Why they are called Catholic Epistles no one knows.[2] Any explanation of the name is an assumption.

Epiphanius (403 A. D.) included the Epistle of Jeremiah and Baruch in his Old Testament.[3]

St. Chrysostom (407 A. D.) did not use Second John, Third John, Second Peter, Jude, and Revelation,[4] all of which are in the Bible now; and in a Synopsis of Scripture attributed to him the canonical list of the Old Testament omits First Chronicles, Second Chronicles, Esther, Job, and Lamentations.[5] We never hear that St. Chrysostom was liable to eternal damnation because he did not "accept the Bible as a whole," or "believe that every word in the blessed book was inspired by God." Another peculiarity of the list is that it repeats Ruth—showing how careless the Fathers could be in stating what was in the sacred volume—and it inserts the Wisdom of Jesus [5] a book which is not now in the Bible.

Theodore, of Mopsuestia, rejected the book of Job, the Epistle of

1 Carm., xii. 31.　　　　　2 Kitto, Cyclo. Bib. Literature—"Epistles, Catholic."
2 Hær., viii. 6.　　　　　　4 Westcott, 438 (410).
5 Ibid., 585 (505).

James, Second Peter, Second John, Third John, Jude, and Revelation,[1] all of which are now in the Bible.

Theodoret, bishop of Cyrus, rejected Second John, Third John, Second Peter, Jude, and Revelation.[2]

There are three great manuscripts of the Greek Bible extant, the Sinaitic, the Vatican, and the Alexandrine. They are the high courts of appeal in all cases of disputed texts, and their lists are, therefore, very important.

The Sinaitic manuscript is one found by Tischendorf in a convent of St. Catharine, Mount Sinai, in 1859, and is probably the oldest of the New Testament codices in existence, dating back to the fourth century. It has the Four Gospels, the Fourteen Epistles of Paul, Acts, the Seven Catholic Epistles, Revelation, the *Epistle of Barnabas*, and a part of the *Shepherd of Hermas*,[3] the last two of which are not in the Bible now.

The Vatican manuscript, in the Vatican library at Rome, belongs to the middle of the fourth century. It ends by mutilation at Hebrews ix. 14. Up to that point it agrees substantially with the Alexandrine manuscript.[4] What other books it may have contained one can not say. The Alexandrine manuscript, belonging to the fifth century, and written probably in Egypt, includes in the Old Testament Tobit Judith, Esdras, First Maccabees, Second Maccabees, Third Maccabees, Fourth Maccabees, the Wisdom of Solomon, and the Wisdom of Jesus, and in the New Testament the two *Epistles of Clement*,[5] none of which are now in our Bible.

---

[1] Westcott, 438, 439 note 1.   [2] Westcott. 439 (411).   [3] Westcott, 426 (396), note 3
[4] Ibid., note 2.   [5] Davidson, Canon, 210 (164); Westcott, 544 (514).

The Clermont Codex, a Latin manuscript now in the Imperial library at Paris, and dating from the fifth to the eighth century, contains a list of the books read in the African Church in the third century.[1] Its Old Testament list omits First Chronicles, Second Chronicles, and Lamentations, which are now in the Bible; and inserts the Wisdom of Solomon, the Wisdom of Jesus son of Sirach, Tobit, Judith, First Maccabees, Second Maccabees, and Third Maccabees, which are not in the Bible. And its New Testament list omits Philippians, First Thessalonians, and Second Thessalonians, which are now in the Bible, and inserts the *Shepherd of Hermas*, the *Acts of Paul*, and the *Revelation of Peter*, which are not now in it.[2] The Epistle which is now called *to the Hebrews* is there called the *Epistle to Barnabas.*[3]

Hilary, of Poitiers, (368 A. D.), included the Epistle of Jeremiah in the Old Testament,[4] although it is not now in the Bible.

Optatus, of Mela, (370 A. D.), omitted Hebrews.[5]

In the early days books were read in the churches which were known at the time to be spurious and which were not in the canon; and finally they obtained a place in the Bible. This was the case with Second Peter. Didymus, of Alexandria, (392 A. D.), says that in his time that book was accounted spurious and was not in the canon, and that yet it was publicly read.[6] To-day it is not only read in the churches, but is accounted genuine and is in the Bible. And if any modern orthodox minister, believing as the ancients did, that it was spurious, desired to say so, he would not dare do it, since it would "unset-

---

[1] Davidson, Canon, 145.   [2] Westcott, Canon, 555, (525).
[3] Ibid., 557, (527) note 1; Davidson, 145. [4] Prol. in Ps., 15.
[5] Davidson, 193.   [6] Westcott, Canon, 444 (416); Davidson, 182 (142).

tle the faith of his congregation." For this he would be dismissed, and the bread and butter of his wife and children would stop. It is thus that ecclesiasticism compels men to play the hypocrite, and teach as true what they believe to be false.

St. Augustine's list (390 A. D.) included Tobit, Judith, First Maccabees, Second Maccabees, Wisdom of Solomon, Ecclesiasticus,[1] which are still in the Catholic Bible but not in the Protestant, and it excluded Lamentations, which is now in both Bibles. His New Testament was the same as ours.[1]

The influence of St. Augustine in establishing the Bible was greater probably than any other Father or than any council. People now attribute to God what was really the work of St. Augustine. While councils decided upon the canon, and their decision became the embodied sentiment of the entire church, the expression was really that of but one man, the leader in the council, and when doubts arose as to the authority of a book, scholarship was not invoked to decide it, for the members possessed almost none. They simply asked. "What did the Early Fathers say of it?" Prof. Davidson says:

"In relation to the New Testament, the synods which drew up lists of the sacred books show the opinion of some leading Father like Augustine, along with what custom had sanctioned. In this department no member of the synod exercised his critical faculty; a number together would decide such questions summarily. Bishops proceeded in the track of tradition or authority.[2]

In 393 A. D. a council met in Hippo, in Africa, discussed the

---

[1] De Doctr. Christ., ii. 13 (M. 1742, p. 41).   [2] Davidson, 172 (134).

canon, and adopted St. Augustine's list.[1] St. Augustine himself was present, and was the ruling spirit.

In 397 A. D. was held the third council of Carthage. St. Augustine was present. It adopted a decree as follows :[2]

"It was also determined that besides the canonical scriptures, nothing be read in the church under the title of Divine Scriptures. The canonical scriptures are these:"

Then follow the names of the books of the Bible as we have them now, except some variations in the order, and except that in the Old Testament list Lamentations is omitted; and the Wisdom of Solomon, Ecclesiasticus, Tobit, Judith, First Maccabees, and Second Maccabees,[2] none of which are now in our Bible, are inserted.

In 419 A. D. another council was held at Carthage, and St. Augustine's list was again ratified.[3]

The reader would err greatly did he suppose that in these assemblies one or two hundred gentlemen sat down to discuss quietly and dignifiedly the questions which had come before them for settlement. On the contrary, many of the bishops were ignorant ruffians, and were followed by crowds of vicious supporters who stood ready on the slightest excuse to maim and kill their opponents. The most shocking scenes that occur in the ward political conventions in the worst districts of our great cities are as nothing compared with what history tells us was common in these Christian councils. Dr. Philip Schaff says:

"Together with abundant talents, attainments, and virtues, there were gathered also at the councils ignorance, intrigues, and partisan passions,

---

[1] Davidson, 189 (148). [2] Westcott, Canon, 436 (408). [3] Davidson,199 (155).

which had already been excited on all sides by long controversies preceding, and now met and arrayed themselves, as hostile armies, for open combat."[1]

Dean Milman, the celebrated historian, says:

"It might have been supposed that nowhere would Christianity appear in such commanding majesty as in a council, which should gather from all quarters of the world the most eminent prelates and the most distinguished clergy; that a lofty and serene piety would govern all their proceedings, and profound and dispassionate investigation exhaust every subject; that human passions and interests would stand rebuked before that awful assembly; that the sense of their own dignity as well as the desire of impressing their brethren with the solemnity and earnestness of their belief would at least exclude all intemperance of manner and language. . . .History shows the melancholy reverse. Nowhere is Christianity less attractive, and if we look to the ordinary tone and character of the proceedings, less authoritative, than in the councils of the church. It is in general a fierce collision of two rival factions, neither of which will yield, each of which is solemnly pledged against conviction. Intrigue, injustice, violence, decisions on authority alone, and that the authority of a turbulent majority, decisions by wild acclamation rather than by sober inquiry, detract from the reverence, and impugn the judgments, at least of the later councils. The close is almost invariably a terrible anathema, in which it is impossible not to discern the tones of human hatred, of arrogant triumph, of rejoicing at the damnation imprecated against the humiliated adversary. . . . The degeneracy is rapid from the council of Nicea to that of Ephesus, where each party came determined to use every means of haste, manœuvre, court influence, bribery, to crush his adversary; where there was an encouragement of, if not an appeal to the violence of the populace, to anticipate the decrees of the council; where each had his own tumultuous foreign rabble to back his quarrel; and neither would scruple at any means to obtain the ratification of their anathemas through persecution by the civil government."[2]

---

[1] History of the Christian Church, by Philip Schaff, D.D., ii. 346 (M 283).

[2] History of Latin Christianity, by H. H. Milman, D.D., i. 226 ff. (New York, 1871), (M 236).

Gregory of Nazianzus, the Christian father, speaks of them as "assemblies of cranes and geese."[1] Utterly disgusted, he declined to have anything to do with them, saying:

"To tell the truth, I am inclined to shun every collection of bishops, because I have never yet seen that a synod came to a good end, or abated evils instead of increasing them. For in those assemblies (and I do not think I express myself too strongly here) indescribable contentiousness and ambition prevail. . . . Therefore I have withdrawn myself, and have found rest to my soul only in solitude."[2]

The third general council of the church, which was held at Ephesus in 431 A. D., was marked by "shameful intrigue, uncharitable lust of condemnation, and coarse violence of conduct."[3] Both factions came with armed escorts, as if going to battle,[4] and were followed by great mobs of the ignorant rabble, slaves and seamen, the lower populace of Constantinople, peasants, and bathmen, and hordes of women, prepared for violence; the city was patrolled by troops,[5] and Nestorius[5] and John of Antioch[6] had armed body guards to protect them from the violence of Cyril's party. The two bands fought in the streets and much blood was shed,[7] and at the reading of the imperial decree such a tumult arose that all the contending bishops were ordered under arrest.[8]

An effort was made immediately after to hold a council in Constantinople, and such was the fear of a riot that it had to be adjourned to the suburban district across the Bosporus.[9]

---

[1] Schaff, History of the Christian Church, ii. 347.
[2] Ep. ad. Procop., 55 old order (al. 130), (Schaff, Hist. Christ. Church, ii. 347).
[3] Schaff, Hist. Christ. Church, ii. 348. [5] Ibid., i. 239   [7] Ibid., i. 240.
[4] Ibid., ii. 723-725. [8] Ibid., i. 242.
[6] Milman, Hist. Latin Christ. i. 230. [9] Ibid., i. 242.

In August, 449 A. D., there met in Ephesus a synod which occupies a notorious place in the scandals of church history, and which, from the fraud and violence by which everything was carried, and the odious character of its proceedings, has received the name of the "Robbers' Council." Dioscorus presided with brutal violence,[1] protected by soldiers. The fear of personal injury was so great that Flavian and his friends, composing one faction, hardly dared to open their lips, while Theodoret was excluded entirely.[1] A communication, presented from Eusebius, was received by the crowd with cries of "Let Eusebius be burnt—let him be burned alive. As he has cut Christ in two, so let him be cut in two."[1] Three delegates from Rome were so terrified, that they did not venture to read an epistle which they bore from Leo.[1] One of the members preferred charges of unchastity against a bishop, but Dioscorus dismissed them with the remark, "If you have an accusation to make against his orthodoxy, we will receive it; but we have not come together to pass judgment concerning unchastity." The subject of the canon was, of course, not the only one discussed by councils. In fact, in many councils it was not referred to. Questions of belief occupied more time than it did. In this council the problem was, "Did Christ have two natures after the incarnation?"[2] In this age, if a man should ask such a question, it would be regarded as the vagary of an unbalanced mind, and hardly compatible with sanity; but the men of that age found it worthy of their most earnest attention. Dioscorus and his party wished Flavian and his friends to sign a confession of faith that Christ had but one

[1] Schaff, Hist. Christ. Church, ii. 738 ff.
[2] Milman, Hist. Latin Christ., i. 288.

nature. Flavian refused to do so. At a given signal the doors were thrown open, a band of soldiers and an armed mob rushed in, and the terrified bishops of the Flavian party were compelled, by blows and at the point of the sword, to sign.[1] Where before there had been two parties there was now not alone a majority, but almost unanimity.[2] The decree having been signed, Dioscorus was no longer able to control his anger, and he struck the vanquished Flavian.[3] Thus encouraged, a crowd of infuriated monks set upon the unfortunate bishop of Jerusalem, crying "Kill him! Kill him!" and they beat and kicked him, and inflicted such injuries that death ensued shortly after.[4] Dean Milman remarks, significantly, that this was not the last council defiled by blood.[5]

Another council, called to meet in Nicea in 451 A. D., was so unruly that it had to be summoned to Chalcedon, across the straits from Constantinople, where the emperor could reach it with his troops and compel order.[6] It is known as the council of Chalcedon. The proceedings were continually interrupted by yells and tumult,[7] and even the laymen were compelled to remind the bishops of their clerical dignity.[7] "At Chalcedon," says Dr. Philip Schaff, "the introduction of the renowned expositor and historian Theodoret provoked a scene which almost involuntarily reminds us of the modern brawls of Greek and Roman monks at the holy sepulchre under the restraining influence of the Turkish police. Theodoret's Egyptian opponents shouted with all their might: 'Away with him, this teacher of Nes-

---

[1] Mosheim, Eccl. Hist., Bk. 2, Cent. 5, pt. 2, ch. v. § 14, note 5, (M 248, i. 481).
[2] Milman, Hist. Latin Christ., i. 288.   [3] Ibid., i. 289.
[4] Ibid., i. 289, Schaff, Hist. Christ. Church., ii. 739.
[5] Hist. Latin Christ., i. 289.
[6] Schaff, Hist. Christ. Church, ii. 742.   [7] Ibid., ii. 743.

torius.' His friends replied with equal violence: 'They forced
us [at the Robber Council] by blows to subscribe, away with
the Manichæans, the enemies of Flavian, the enemies of the faith.
Away with the murderer Dioscorus. Who does not know his
wicked deeds?' The Egyptian bishops cried again: 'Away with
the Jew, the adversary of God, and call him not bishop.' To
which the oriental bishops answered: 'Away with the rioters,
away with the murderers! The orthodox man belongs to the
council.'" The military had to interfere to quell the proceedings.[1]

At a council held at Constantinople in 785 A. D., the soldiery
burst into the chamber and dispersed the affrighted bishops
because they did not approve of the bishops' enactments;[2] and
the second council of Nicea (787 A. D.) denounced this council of Constantinople as a synod of fools and madmen.[3]

There is one curious fact to which I can not refrain from
calling attention. No Christian historian, whether Mosheim,
Milman, Schaff, or any other, has ever perceived, apparently,
the grotesque absurdity of an assembly attempting to decide
by vote a fact in the past. Men vote on questions which have
yet to be decided, and thus make them facts—as whether this
man or that man shall be president, or this law or that shall
be in force—but not on those which are already decided. That
Christian councils ever seriously discussed "Did Christ have
two natures or one after incarnation?" is of itself almost anom-
alous. But to say nothing of that—to attempt to decide it by a
vote is like trying to decide by a vote whether or not he was

---

[1] Hist. Christ. Church, ii. 348, see also ibid., ii. 742, and Milman, Hist.
Latin Christ., i. 291 ff.
[2] Milman, ii. 345.   [3] Ibid., ii. 346.

crucified. If he had two natures he had two, and the fact could not be made to depend on a vote taken five hundred years afterwards. Yet all the "great Christian historians" discuss such things with the utmost naïveté, and never for a moment perceive their absurdity. This is only one instance in many which might be cited, wherein these gentlemen almost forfeit the patience of intelligent skeptics. They devote time in all seriousness to simple nonsense, and overlook the facts lying all about them which completely overwhelm the Christian theology with defeat.

Having learned the character of the councils, let us return to the canon.

Jerome (420 A. D.) said that Wisdom, Sirach, Judith, Tobit, and the books of Maccabees, were not in the Bible.[1] In the New Testament he included Hebrews and Revelation on the authority of the ancient writers, and not of the existing custom,[2] showing that in his time they were frequently rejected. In another work he gave the Epistle of Barnabas at the end of a canonical list, and he expresses the doubts in existence as to Philemon, Second Peter, Jude, Second John, and Third John,[2] of which, to-day, no doubts are entertained. The First Epistle of Clement, which is not now in the Bible, was, he says, read in some churches.[2] His reasons for excluding the apocryphal books of the Old Testament were:

"Both the Syriac and Chaldaic languages testify that there are twenty-two letters in the Hebrew alphabet. . . . Moreover, there are five double letters, . . . whence it is also thought by many that there are five double books, Samuel, Kings, Chronicles, Ezra with Nehemiah, and Jeremiah with Lamentations. In the same way, therefore, as there are twenty-two elements by

[1] Intro. Sam. and Kings.   [2] Davidson, 190 ff.

which we write all Hebrew which we speak, so there are twenty-two volumes, by which letters, as it were, the beginner is instructed in the doctrine of God."[1]

This superstition was entertained by many of the Hebrew and early Christian theologians. Jerome's method of reckoning was as follows: The Pentateuch was counted five books; Judges and Ruth, which were originally one book, the two being called Judges, were considered one; the ten books cited above were called five "double" books; Hosea, Joel, Amos, Obadiah, Jonah, Micah, Nahum, Habakkuk, Zephaniah, Haggai, Zechariah, and Malachi, twelve in all, were called one, according to the ancient custom; and each of the remaining books, one. The present age does not approve of such a means of establishing a theory, but to the theological intellect, endowed with "spiritual insight," nothing is absurd. This is the reason why the Protestant Bible has to-day fewer books than the Catholic. The two men most influential in determining the canon were Augustine and Jerome.[2] The Catholic Church has followed the former, and Luther and the reformers followed the latter. As to their qualifications for deciding the canon Prof. Davidson says:

"Both were unfitted for the critical examination of such a topic. The former was a gifted spiritual man, lacking learning and independence. Tradition dominated all his ideas about the difficult or disputed books. . . . His judgment was weak, his sagacity moderate, and the absence of many-sidedness hindered a critical result. Jerome, again, was learned but timid, lacking the courage to face the question fairly or fundamentally, and the in-

---

[1] Intro. Samuel and Kings. The desire to see a mystery in numbers finds a curious illustration in the confession of Metrophanes Critopulus, where it is said that the Bible should contain "thirty-three books in all, equal in number to the years of our Savior's life." [Westcott, Canon, 435 (407) note.]

[2] Davidson. Canon, 233.

dependence necessary to its right investigation. Belonging as he did to both churches, he recommended the practice of the one to the other. He, too, was chiefly influenced by tradition."[1]

The canons in the Apostolic Constitutions[2] omit from the New Testament James, First Peter, Second Peter, First John, Second John, Third John, Jude and Revelation.[3] This is the more remarkable from the fact that the canon prescribes with great particularity and minuteness how services in church should be conducted, and what books should be read.

The catalogue in the eighty-fifth of the Apostolic canons includes in the Old Testament the Wisdom of Jesus, Judith, First Maccabees, Second Maccabees, and Third Maccabees,[4] which are not now a part of the Bible. As to the New, it omits Revelation, and includes the *First Epistle of Clement*, the *Second Epistle of Clement* (an acknowledged forgery), and the *Clementine Constitutions*.[4] No one ever hears of these books being included in the New Testament now. It is a noteworthy fact that this and the preceding list, contradictory as they are, are both in the same book.

Cosmas Indicopleustes (535 A.D.) never mentions James, First Peter, Second Peter, First John, Second John, Third John, Jude, or Revelation.[1] Cosmas is the man who asked exultingly, if

---

[1] Davidson, Canon, 200 (155).

[2] The Apostolic Constitutions are a collection of rules, mainly for the guidance of the clergy. They date from the fifth century, and are not to be attributed to the Apostles, their name being another of the many of similar endeavors to give authority to books by forging great names to them.

[3] Apostolic Constitutions, II, 57 (M 1733, p. 84).

[4] Ibid., VIII, xlvii. 85 (M 1733, p. 268).

the world were round how the people on the other side were
to see the Lord Jesus descending through the air on the last
great day.[2]

Junilius, an African Bishop, (550 A. D.), divided the books of
the Bible into those *perfect*, those of *intermediate*, and those of
no authority. The first class included the Wisdom of Jesus,
which is not now in the Bible. The second included First
Chronicles, Second Chronicles, Job, Ezra, Nehemiah, Judith,
Esther, First Maccabees, Second Maccabees, of the Old Testament; and James, Second Peter, Jude, Second John, and Third
John, of the New, all of which we consider as authoritative as
any. The third included the Wisdom of Solomon and the Song
of Solomon, the former of which is not and the latter of which
is in the Bible to-day. He added that the Revelation of John
was doubted by many in the East.[3]

By the year 629 A. D. so diverse had become the views as to
what should compose the Bible, and so great was the need of
harmony, that the sixth general council of Constantinople,
otherwise known as the Quinisextine or Trullan council, with a
desire apparently to please all parties, ratified the catalogues
of Laodicea and Carthage, the Apostolic canons, and those of
Athanasius, Gregory of Nazianzus, Amphilochius of Iconium,
Cyril of Alexandria,[4] and every other one of which they had
any knowledge, seemingly indifferent to the absurdity of indors-
ing the contradictions between them. All these lists are virtually comprehended in the Laodicean, the Carthaginian and
the Apostolic, and the custom is to say that the council ratified

---

[1] Davidson, Canon, 212.   [2] Draper, Intellectual Development, ii. 159.
[3] De partibus divinæ legis, i. 2 [Davidson 205].   [4] Davidson, 235.

those three.[1] No two of these catalogues were alike, and the following table shows the differences between them. The letters "in" signify that the book was included in the list, and "om" that it was omitted. It will be observed that out of fourteen books, some are in two but none are in the three lists.

BOOKS.	LAODICEAN.	CARTHAGINIAN.	APOSTOLIC.
Lamentations	in	om	in
Epistle of Jeremiah	in	om	om
Judith	om	in	in
1 Maccabees	om	in	in
2 Maccabees	om	in	in
3 Maccabees	om	om	in
Wisdom of Solomon	om	in	om
Tobit	om	in	om
Baruch	in	om	om
Wisdom of Jesus	om	in	in
Revelation	om	in	om
First Epistle of Clement	om	om	in
Second Epistle of Clement	om	om	in
Apostolic Constitutions	om	om	in

It should be added that at this council the Clementine Constitutions, though in the Apostolic catalogue, and recognized by the assembly as authoritative, were declared to be no longer canonical, on account of the interpolations which they had received.[2]

At the fourth council of Toledo (632 A. D.) Augustine's list was again ratified.[3]

Johannes Damascenus (750 A. D.) gives as the New Testa-

[1] Westcott, Canon, 434 (406), 440 (412), note 4.
[2] Westcott, 434 (406).   [3] Davidson, 237.

ment all the books now in it and the Apostolic Constitutions.[1]
He omits Lamentations from the Old Testament.[1]

Nicephorus (about 810 A. D.) included in his Old Testament
list Baruch, and he excluded Esther, asserting positively that
it was among the books not to be received. He excluded from
his New Testament Revelation, and placed it on a level with
the *Revelation of Peter*, the *Epistle of Barnabas*, and the *Gospel according to the Hebrews.*[2]

Photius, Œcumenius and Theophylact rejected Revelation.[3]
Alfric, Abbot of Cerne, (989 A. D.), said the Bible consisted of
the Four Gospels, the Seven Catholic Epistles, fifteen Epistles
of Paul including Hebrews and the *Epistle to the Laodiceans*,
the Acts, and Revelation.[4] The Epistle to the Laodiceans here
mentioned has a curious history. Paul says in his Epistle to
the Colossians (iv. 16) that he had written a letter to the
Laodiceans, and an Epistle claiming to be that one was in circulation in the second century.[5] The one now under discussion, which is a different book from that one, begins as all the
genuine Epistles do, "Paul, an apostle not of men, nor by men,
but by Jesus Christ, to the brethren that be at Laodicea," etc.
The earliest trace of it is at the beginning of the sixth century.
Gregory the Great, at the close of that period, declared it was
written by Paul. Haymo, Bishop of Halberstadt, (853 A. D.),
did the same. So did John of Salisbury not long after. The
opinion of Alfric confirmed these, and the Epistle passed into
the early translations of the New Testament. It is in the
Speculum published by Mai, and in the manuscript of the Vul-

---

[1] De Fide Orthodoxa, iv. 17.   [3] Westcott, 552 (522); Davidson, 211.
[3] Westcott, 446 (418).   [4] Westcott, 452 (424).   [5] Ibid., 455 (427).

gate Bible at La Cava. It is in the manuscript of the Latin New Testament which is still preserved at Fulda; in very many western manuscripts of the Bible, as in the great Gothic Bible of Toledo, (eighth century), in the Book of Armagh (807 A. D.), in the so-called Charlemagne's Bible of the British museum (ninth century), in the great Bible of the king's library in the British museum, apparently designed for church use, and in many other magnificent Bibles. Fourteen editions of one or more German versions of it are said to have been printed before Luther's time; it is in the first Bohemian Bible (1488), and it is in the Albigensian Bible at Lyons, where it has its usual place after the Epistle to the Colossians.[1] From the sixth to the sixteenth century, a thousand years, this Epistle was in the Bible of a large share of the Christian people; and yet we now never even hear of it, much less do we hear it called the word of God.

Henry I., Count of Champagne, (1165 A. D.), wrote to John of Salisbury secretary to Thomas à Beckett, asking him how many books there really were in the Bible, and who were their authors. To this John replied, giving the list as we have it to-day, but including also the Epistle to the Laodiceans just referred to.[2] He adds concerning the canon, "I consider that it is not of much importance either to me or to others what opinion be held. For whether we hold this opinion or that, it brings no damage to our salvation. But to indulge in a fierce controversy on a subject which is either indifferent in its result or of little moment, is as bad as a sharp discussion about goat's wool between friends." This illustrates what I have already

---

[1] Westcott, 454 (426) ff.   [2] Ibid., 459 (431).

alluded to, that among many of the Fathers the question as to what was in the Bible was of very small importance. The idea of the Bible, such as we have now, they never dreamed of.

A singular canon was that of Ebed Jesu, (1318 A. D.), a Nestorian bishop. He gave, he said, a list of the "divine books" and "all the ecclesiastical compositions." In his Old Testament he included Ecclesiasticus, the Wisdom of Solomon, Judith, the Story of Susanna, the Lesser Daniel, and Baruch, which are not now in the Bible; and without any break to indicate where the Biblical books end and the ecclesiastical books begin, he adds the books of the Traditions of the Elders (the Mishna), the works of Josephus, the fables of Esoph, the history of the Sons of Samonas, the book of Maccabees, the history of King Herod, the book of the Last Desolation of Jerusalem by Titus, the book of Asiatha, wife of Joseph, the just son of Jacob, and the book of Tobias and Tobit. Apparently he did not know that Tobias and Tobit were the same book. From his New Testament he excluded Second Peter, Second John, Third John, Jude, and Revelation, all of which are now in the Bible, (let the reader remember that this was so late as the fourteenth century), and he adds, presumably as ecclesiastical, the Diatessaron of Tatian, the books of the Disciples of the Apostles, the book of Dionysius "the divine philosopher," and the books of Clement.[1] It is very evident that the idea of a Bible such as we entertain he did not have.

---

[1] Westcott, 538 (508).

A council of Florence (1441) adopted the list which the council of Trent subsequently reiterated.[1]

We come now to the reformation. For thirteen hundred years the church had been endeavoring to harmonize on a Bible by permitting the bishops and ecclesiastics to settle the matter generally among themselves, and it had resulted only in violent clashing of opinion. An ominous revolt was breaking out in the North. Luther was pushing the claim of the right of private judgment to its utmost. And as the Bible was the key of the situation, the church, which had been growing more and more restrictive and had thus accumulated precedent for its proposed step, took the whole question of the canon in hand, fixed it once for all, and forbade any individual to have anything further to do with it. The council of Trent met Dec. 13, 1545, and on Feb. 12, 1546, the question of the canon was brought forward. Luther had declared that the Bible alone was the source of authority. The Church declared tradition to be of equal authority. Luther declared that the universally accepted books of the Old and New Testament, without any of the apocryphal or disputed books, should alone constitute the Bible. The church wanted the apocrypha admitted. The questions were discussed in the council by about thirty ecclesiastics in four sessions. For the second time in the history of the book came a compromise. Four factions were contending for the adoption of different views. All were agreed that tradition—hearsay, rumor—was of equal authority with written records. The grotesque misnomer of calling such men "great." or "scholars," is quite apparent. On the subject concerning

[1] Davidson, 245 (178).

which there should have been division, there was unity; and on the one on which there should have been unity, there was division. One party desired two classes of books, as St. Augustine had divided them, the canonical and uncanonical; the second desired three classes, the acknowledged books, the disputed books of the New Testament, and the apocryphal books of the Old Testament, in each case, of course, the uncanonical books to be thrown out; the third party desired the list simply to be named, without anything being said as to the authority of the books, as had been done at the third council of Carthage; and the fourth demanded that all the books, acknowledged, disputed, and apocryphal, should be classed together, and the whole called of divine authority. As is generally the case in a religious council where "spiritual insight" is permitted to rule, stupidity gained the day. The first and second parties combined about March 8, but notwithstanding this, on the 15th the third party secured a majority, and the following decree was adopted:

"The holy œcumenical and general council of Trent, . . . following the examples of the orthodox Fathers, receives and venerates all the books of the Old and New Testaments, . . . and also traditions pertaining to faith and conduct, . . . with an equal feeling of devotion and reverence. . . . The synod thought proper, therefore, to annex to this decree a catalogue of the sacred books, lest any doubt might arise concerning those that were approved of. They are the following: [Then are given the names of the books exactly as they stand in the Catholic Bible to-day, and the decree proceeds.] Now, if any one reading over these books in all their parts, as they are usually read in the Latin Vulgate edition, does not hold them for sacred and canonical [observe "canonical," not "inspired"] and, knowing the aforesaid traditions, does industriously contemn them, let him be anathema."[1]

[1] The facts here narrated will be found in Westcott, Canon, 472 (444) ff. The decree will also be found in Schaff's Creeds of Christendom, ii. 79.

That is where the doctrine originated that we must believe the Bible or be damned. More than one thousand five hundred years after Jesus Christ was dead, the superstition arose. And the Catholic Church does not yet insist on inspiration, for it holds to the authority of tradition, and gossip and inspiration do not always agree. But who were the men that established this damnation theory of the Bible?

"This fatal decree—in which the council, harassed by the fear of lay critics and 'grammarians,' gave a new aspect to the whole question of the canon—was ratified by fifty-three prelates, among whom there was not . . . one scholar distinguished for historical learning, not one who was fitted by special study for the examination of a subject in which the truth could alone be determined by the voice of antiquity."[1]

That was the character of the men who said that their work was the work of God. For—let the reader remember—the books in the Catholic Bible are not what God said should be there, but what these men said should be. God had nothing to do with it. Furthermore, this was the first time in the history of the church that anything which had been before simply a matter of custom and opinion, was made a belief to be accepted on pain of eternal damnation,[2] and it has been the unfortunate parent of a most numerous and hideous progeny. Having once a precedent for declaring endless punishment a penalty for non-belief in dogmas not taught in the Bible, a whole brood of superstitions followed and have been current to this day.

This practically settled the question of the canon in the Catholic Church.[3] A few men, later, protested, and endeavored to revise the list,[4] but the struggle was useless.

[1] Westcott, 474 (446). [2] Ibid. [3] Davidson, 237. [4] Westcott, 475 (447).

To complete the absurdity, the Eastern Church, which had for one thousand three hundred years declared persistently that Revelation was not written by John and was not entitled to a place in the Bible, wheeled squarely about, and in a council held in Jerusalem in 1672, adopted the decree of Trent,[1] Revelation and all, and to-day considers Revelation as much the word of God as any other book!

The reformers went further, and made the idea of inspiration take the place of canonicity.[2]

Now, mark the beginning of the belief in the Bible which we hold to-day. The Protestant Church is a book-worshipper. It makes a fetich of a book. The Catholics care little for the Bible, and ever have. They say, "Take away the whole book if you like, and the church will still remain in all its power. The book is the creation of the church, not the church the creation of the book." The Protestants, finding themselves confronted with an infallible church, had to oppose it with an infallible book. And they made a book infallible, which before had not been considered so. And well they might, for they were compelled to. It is commonly the case that the overthrow of one superstition is only accomplished by the establishment of another in its place. By friction and contrast the two will in time wear each other away. But those minds have been exceedingly few which could reject a theology and retain the calm equipoise, the philosophical attitude of non-belief in any. The Catholics had the prestige of antiquity, and of being considered the only true Church of God, and they threatened with eternal damnation every man who followed Luther. The masses of the people of the North, ignorant and supersti-

[1] Davidson, 246 (179).   [2] Westcott, 487 (459).

tious, were naturally terrified and cowed by the awful threat, and the only wonder is that they ever stood before the storm. To meet it, Luther, Calvin and others said that the Bible was *supernaturally* inspired. The origin of the books having been forgotten, men, credulous and in trouble, came to think that because the books were written of God they were written by God. The reformers declared that the Bible and not the church was the sole source of authority. This succeeded, and the thunders of the Vatican were answered by the thunders of artillery. Armies swept across the face of Europe, and it was amid the roar of cannon, the shock of battle, and the shrieks of the dying, that the doctrine of the divine and infallible inspiration of the Bible grew. That this is so, and that the idea arose with men who were in the highest state of fanaticism, is illustrated by the following decree, adopted by the Calvinistic council of Switzerland in 1675:

"Almighty God not only provided that his word, which is a power to every one who believes, should be committed to writing through Moses, the Prophets, and Apostles, but also has watched over it with a fatherly care up to the present time, and guarded lest it might be corrupted by the craft of Satan or any fraud of men. . . . The Hebrew volume of the Old Testament, which we have received from the tradition of the Jewish church—to which formerly the oracles of God were committed—and retain at the present day, both in its consonants and in its vowels, the points themselves, or at least the force of the points, and both in its substance and its words is divinely inspired, so that, together with the volume of the New Testament, it is the single and uncorrupted rule of our faith and life, by whose standard, as by a touchstone, all versions which exist, whether Eastern or Western, must be tried, and wherever they vary, be made conformable to it."[1]

[1] Niemeyer Collectio Confessionum, 730.

Three things indicate the grim ferocity of this dogma; 1, It says that God has guarded the Bible from corruption; yet Griesbach collected *one hundred and fifty thousand* various readings in the New Testament manuscripts alone,[1] the greater part of which must, of course, be corruptions, since there can be but one correct reading for any passage. 2, It says the vowels were inspired, whereas the ancient Hebrew literature had no vowels. And 3, It says that the vowel-points were inspired; whereas they did not come into use until the seventh century after Jesus, and were not perfected until four centuries later. This last article is a relic of that ancient belief that the translators, the copyists, and all the men who had aught to do with the transmission of the Bible from century to century, were inspired.

The Belgian Confession (1561-63 A. D.) affords another curious illustration of the highly wrought mental condition of that time. It says: "We embrace the Holy Scripture in those two volumes of the Old and New Testament, which are called the canonical books, *about which there is no controversy.*"[2] Then follows a list of the books of the Bible as we receive them now, including also the books which, the reader has seen, had been in controversy for fifteen hundred years, and were even then. And notwithstanding these facts the italicised words were subsequently changed to read "about which there never was any controversy."![2] The creed proceeds, "And we

---

[1] Genuineness and Authenticity of the Gospels, by B. A. Hinsdale, M. A., President of Hiram College, O., Cincinnati, 1872, p. 130; Anglo-American Bible Revision, 91, (M 41).

[2] Niemeyer, Collectio Confessionum, pp. 361-363, Art. 3-7; Westcott, 488 (460); Schaff, Creeds of Christendom, iii. 385. The italics are mine.

believe all those things contained in them, . . . because the Holy Spirit witnesses to our consciences that they emanated from God."[1] We are told by theologians that we can not trust to the reason, that we must 'experience the testimony of the spirit' to believe the doctrines of the church. and that that testimony can be relied upon. Yet here we find a people offering the 'testimony of the spirit' to the truth of a thing which we now know to be false. The 'testimony of the spirit' is a mental delusion. The Christian no doubt thinks he has it. He is honest in it, but he mistakes. There is no such thing. His imagination supplies his facts, just as is the case with a man suffering from delirium tremens, who thinks he sees various hideous creatures. Religious enthusiasm—such as says that "every word in the blessed Bible was inspired by God"—is a mental and moral delirium tremens.

The Protestants, however, though convinced that the Bible was infallibly inspired, had their difficulties in determining what the Bible really was. And the fierceness with which they insisted on their views ended in the suppression of all historical criticism.[2] Erasmus (1467—1536 A. D.) said that Hebrews was not written by Paul, nor Second John and Third John by the Apostle, but by another John; nor Revelation by John.[3] He was the literary leader of the Reformation. While he was still a Catholic, an attack was made on his views by the Sarbonne, the theological faculty of Paris; censure was placed on his doubts, and it was declared that, no matter if

---

[1] Niemeyer, Collectio Confessionum, pp. 361-363, Art. 3-7; Westcott, 488 (460), Schaff, Creeds of Christendom, iii. 385.
[2] Westcott, 465 (437).   [3] Westcott, 467 (439) ff.

the genuineness of certain books had been disputed in ancient times, the fact that the church had since accepted them made it wrong for any Christian to dispute them.[1]

Bodenstein, of Karlstadt, (1520 A. D.), the reformer, and the great friend but finally the persecuted enemy of Luther, divided the books of the Bible into three classes. In the first he placed the Pentateuch and the Four Gospels; in the second, as of less authority, the Prophets of the Old Testament and the "acknowledged" Epistles of the New Testament (i. e., thirteen of Paul, First Peter, and First John); and in the third class, as of least authority, the Hagiographa of the Old Testament, and Hebrews, James, Second Peter, Second John, Third John, Jude, and Revelation, of the New.[2] He omitted the book of Acts entirely.[3]

Luther thought First Maccabees almost equal to the other books of Holy Scripture and not unworthy to be reckoned among them.[4] It is not reckoned among them now by Protestants. Of Wisdom he says he was long in doubt whether it should be numbered among the canonical books,[5] and of Sirach that it was a right good book, proceeding from a wise man.[6] He thought the book of Esther should not belong to the canon.[7] It is there now, however. He said that Hebrews was written by neither Paul nor an apostle, and he did not place it on equality with the epistles written by the apostles. He thought it was a compilation from pre-existing records, and while it had much in it that was good, it also had "wood, straw, or

---

[1] Westcott, 470 (442).   [2] De Canonis Scripturis.   [3] Ibid., §§ 65 ff.
[4] Pref. 1 Macc.   [5] Pref. Wisdom.
[6] Pref. Ecclus.   [7] Pref. Esther.

hay" in its composition.[1] James was, he said, an epistle of straw, with no character of the Gospel in it; it was not written by any apostle, and was not a true Bible book.[2] The Epistle of Jude was, he declared, a reprint from Second Peter (if the reader will compare the second chapter of Second Peter and the first part of the third chapter with the Epistle of Jude, he will see that they closely resemble each other) and therefore it did not, in his opinion, belong among the canonical books.[3] Revelation he considered neither prophetic nor apostolic, and thought that it was almost on a level with the fourth book of Esdras, which last he proposed to throw into the river Elbe.[4] He modified this view twelve years later so far as to say that it was a dumb prophecy, and that there was no objection to any one believing it to have been written by the Apostle John, who desired to do so.[5] As for himself he did not believe it. He placed Hebrews, James, Jude and Revelation in an appendix to his New Testament, as of inferior authority.[6]

Zwingli (1531 A. D.) declared that he took no account of Revelaton, for it was not a book of the Bible.[7] Œcolampadius (1531 A. D.) said that the Protestants of Switzerland did not compare James, Jude, Second Peter, Second John, Third John, and Revelation, with the other books of the Bible.[8] Calvin, on the other hand, said that though Hebrews was not written by Paul, it was through a Satanic device that its authority had been questioned,[9] and that Second Peter, though not written by Peter, was written by some disciple at his command.[1]

[1] Pref. Epis. ad Heb.
[2] Pref. Epis. Judæ.
[5] Westcott, 479 (451), and note 2.
[7] Works, ed. Schuler II, i. 169.
[9] Pref. Heb.
[3] Pref. Epis. Jacobi.
[4] Davidson, 216 (171).
[6] Westcott, 477 (449).
[8] Epis., i. 3, c., ed. 1548.

He passed over Second John, Third John, and Revelation, without any notice in his commentary.

Luther and his successors, it will be seen, made the same distinction between the New Testament books that had been made between those of the Old Testament, classifying them according to the "generally received" and the "controverted." It was the council of Trent which obliterated the distinction between the books of the Old Testament, and the Calvinists who obliterated it between the books of the New.[2] The Lutherans also discarded subsequently Luther's views, and accepted all the books as of equal authority, and thus all over the Protestant world the books of the canon were placed on the same level.

Finally, the Westminister assembly in 1647 adopted a list which has since been accepted by the Presbyterians of England, Ireland and America, the Congregationalists of both countries, and, in short, by the Protestant evangelical and orthodox churches with which we come in contact in our daily life in the United States. It is in the famous Westminister Confession, is the one now in our Bibles, and is the same as the Catholic list except that it rejects the Old Testament apocrypha.[3] The latter was, however, for a long time printed in an appendix, and some who read this, especially elderly persons, can remember seeing the apocrypha in the old family Bibles. But in 1827 the British and Foreign Bible Society decided that it would no longer circulate those books,[4] the American Bible

---

[1] Pref. 2 Peter.
[2] Davidson, Canon, 217 (171).
[3] Schaff, Creeds of Christendom, iii. 601 (M 1277).
[4] Lange, Comm., xv. 56 ff., Am. ed., 1880, (M 120).

Society followed its example,[1] and thus it was that our Bible received its finishing touch, as we have been accustomed to see it.

RÉSUMÉ.—In taking a brief review of the subject, we find that the greater number of the books of the Bible are anonymous. No one knows who wrote them, and no one knows when they were written. They are, in the cases of the most important books, of those most relied on for doctrinal support, compilations from pre-existing records. But who wrote those records, and who made the compilations, are entirely unknown. When the books of the Old Testament came into use they were not considered inspired. That idea was an afterthought. And the Christian Church places a higher value on some of the books than the original possessors or than Jesus himself did. In the same manner, when the books of the New Testament came into use they were not considered inspired or the word of God. Many Gospels, Epistles and Revelations, not now in use, were read in the churches in the early centuries. About the close of the second century or the beginning of the third, when the Catholic Church was forming, a source of authority for appeal in case of dispute over new doctrines was necessary, and the Fathers instituted the theory that certain books were inspired. But the books which they said were divine were not always the same books which we have now. They declared many books to be inspired which we do not think to be; and they ignored and rejected many books which have since been invested with divine honors. The contentions of the sects made it impossible for the new church to unite on

[1] Schaff, Bible Dict., "Apocrypha."

the Gospels which had been first in use, and they were, there-fore, discarded, and our present Four Gospels were substi-tuted. To give them greater authority, the names of apostles who had been with Jesus were forged to them, literary forgery in those days not being considered a crime. The Fathers in asserting that the books were inspired, were guided not by critical ability, but by ignorance and superstition. Instead of being great scholars, they were extremely credulous, and in general very inferior intellectually. After much controversy, it became apparent that they could not agree as to what books should form the Bible; and councils took the matter in hand, and for nearly twelve centuries they discussed it. And finally, the Roman Catholic Church in the council of Trent, and the Greek Church in the council of Constantinople, decided once for all what the list should be for their adherents; and the Westminster Assembly gave the English-speaking Protestants their catalogue.

The Bible, as we have it to-day, is hardly more than three centuries old.

INDEX

Printed in the United States
1203700005B/183-186